"Donna has written a powerful, authentic, vulnerable and
pain, this is an incredible way to support your healing." ~

"Donna DeNomme has pulled out all of the stops! This book is filled with deep soul truths, shamanic wisdom,
practical insights, and healing practices. What a gem!" ~ Dianne Fresquez, owner of For Heaven's Sake Books

"I haven't had experience of abuse so I was quite surprised that 8 Keys has such a universal message. It goes
way beyond physical abuse and encourages readers to address anything in their lives that blocks living a full
and positive life, without blame. With so many insights and deep wisdom, it's a truly worthwhile read."
~ Susan Andra Lion, award-winning graphic designer and illustrator, author of How the Trees Got Their Voices

"I felt swept up and fully engaged . . . . This book shares from a deeply personal perspective of healing and
awakening, while also offering useful tools and practices designed for clearing old patterns, and bringing balance
and restoration to our daily lives." ~ Carl Studna, photographer and author of CLICK! Choosing Love, One Frame at a Time

"This is a stunning piece of work!" ~ Karen Stuth, publisher and founder of Satiama

"Donna DeNomme's honesty and insight will open the soul and guide the heart through the hard walk to
wholeness. She dares to speak a truth that will liberate so many others who will know they are not walking
alone, and her keys will illuminate their path."
~ Fawn Germer, international speaker and best-selling author of Hard Won Wisdom

"This is the type of experience that lingers and teaches beyond the time and the space in which it was presented.
The work that you do happens on so many other levels, not just in the intellect . . . the bargain is that people
have an opportunity to get infinitesimally more than they came for."
~ Rev. Mary Jo Honiotes, Spiritual Director at the Center for Spiritual Living: Denver

"Donna DeNomme is a gifted writer and powerful spiritual practitioner. Her book, 8 Keys to Wholeness –
Tools for Hope-Filled Healing, provides inspiration and clear direction for self-discovery, comfort, and true
transformation. Her compassion and her connection with Spirit make her a tremendous blessing and an
inspiration for moving through trauma and moving forward in life. Read it, share it with others, and enjoy
more of the great life you deserve." ~ Dr. Roger Teel, Spiritual Leader, Mile Hi Church, Denver, Colorado

"Donna's experience and expertise sheds light on multi-dimensional healing—working from the heart center,
yet radiating through all the chakras. Practically educational and imminently personal, this book will help you
cleanse your physical, emotional, and energetic bodies and may play an unprecedented role in uplifting the
wider spiritual and cultural communities. A powerful and empowering read!"
~ Rasamayi, yogini, teacher, and internationally-renowned sound healing musician

"Your grasp of all the dimensions of this issue really opens it in a way that I don't think anyone else has."
~ Dara Marks, top Hollywood script consultant, author of Inside Story

"Donna, this is all so powerful—you are such a wonderful writer, a radiant being and teacher! Love your story
of hope." ~ Janis Page, counselor and teacher

"You are a Spiritual Warrior." ~ Dr. Susan Rowland, author of Jung: A Feminist Revision

8 Keys to Wholeness

Tools for Hope-Filled Healing

Donna DeNomme
Master Success Coach

Inlightened Source Publishing
18719 W. 60th Ave
Golden, Colorado 80403

LCCN: 2013919398
ISBN: 978-0-9848589-5-8 print
ISBN: 978-0-9848589-8-9 ebook

Cover and interior design: Sue Lion
Illustrations: Sue Lion, www.suelion.com
Back cover photo: Carl Studna, www.carlstudna.com
Editor: Cara Cantarella

Printed in the U.S. by United Graphics Incorporated

Self-Help / Abuse & Trauma / Motivational / Inspirational / Chakra / Healing

The Path Leads Home

Something eternal, something with greater meaning,

begins to shine through the dark veil of earthly existence.

~ Marie-Louise von Franz[1]

We can never really escape ourselves.

~ Donna DeNomme

I have been told that I needed to write about my past. There is no way, I thought . . . .

But some things in our lives go beyond our personal choice to a greater purpose. It was through a strange and synchronistic series of events, like with most of life's grand schemes, that I found myself writing with an abandon that navigated around all of my resistance, and the greater purpose made itself known.

The first opening peeked through four years ago during a meditation welcoming in the new year[2], when I spontaneously, and distinctly, felt and "saw" two exquisite white birds rise from deep within my High Heart. They stretched and moved through my throat, pushing their way forcibly out through my mouth, flying freely airborne as I heard a voice of conviction say,

"Your wound has become your strength."

Dear Reader,

I am really good at keeping secrets. People trust me with their deepest, darkest thoughts. And whether they are clients or friends, I do not breech their confidence. I learned to bury secrets long ago, leaving them untouched and intact, alive beneath the surface of what I showed to the outer world.

The story in this book is real. I did not consciously decide to share it, but instead, through a series of odd circumstances, it became clear that it was time. While searching for a structure to hold what was difficult, a vision presented itself with soothing and encouraging imagery—a magnificent rainbow grew out of the empty darkness, and I embraced its looming brilliance as my strength. The image of the rainbow became the sacred vessel for my words.

We find the rainbow symbolic, as it relates to the individual, in the form of the energetic chakra system that strives to find balance and harmony within each of us, and also as the large rainbow arc seen after a violent storm, connecting heaven with earth. The rainbow inspires an illumination understood in both the indigenous Rainbow Warrior teachings and the Pachakuti Mesa tradition: that we are all one people, and that we must, for the sake of the planet, find our collective balance like the rays of the rainbow. The Great Mystery, which is life itself, guides us in this endeavor in remarkable ways. Through the 8 Keys to Wholeness, which relate to energy centers that are always present because we carry them with us wherever we are, we can create lasting, hope-filled healing and true transformation.

No one of us holds the answer for another. Yet, as a spiritual coach and teacher, I have assisted many people as they moved through their pain. As a shamanic practitioner, I have facilitated expansive spiritual journeys, as well as integrative rituals, to create lasting shifts. It is my privilege to offer support to you. Through offering a soul-centered weaving meant to evoke the heart to partner with the mind, my desire is for you to discover, or reconnect with, those banished fragments of what is difficult to look at, painful to hold. When we walk into and through trauma, facing our pain and fears, we find precious gifts and treasures hidden within.

In preparation for this writing, a surprising sense of gentle peace came during my most gruesome research—research exposing shockingly brutal pieces that validated my memory and gave permission to my stifled voice. Life comes together in a way that fiction cannot. Although parts of what I share may seem difficult to comprehend, all that is contained here is the truth as I know it to be. Events are not told in chronological order, but instead fall within the parameters of the keys to which they relate and rightfully portray.

Whether or not you identify with my particular story, I encourage you to be open to what perspective it may offer for your own. In the sacred tradition of the healer, who offers her personal pain in sacrifice for the good of the tribe, I muster the boldness to lay my own ugliness bare before you, clearly speaking what for me has been unspeakable. I suggest that you do not get stuck in the surface of the story—mine or yours—but explore the transformative portals unlocked by the 8 Keys, which have the power to lead you to personal insight and true transformation. These Keys open us to the ways and means to integrate wounds into a fuller and richer Wholeness.

Each of us experiences pain in one form or another, and everyone's pain matters. Our ultimate task is to learn to trust both the smooth, open path and the jagged crevices that life brings. Like hikers in the wilderness, we can learn to read subtle markings that show us how to navigate our way home. Through all of life's twists and turns, we are provided with so many precious opportunities for personal growth. Life is "for" (not against) us! Healing is the great, undeniable force that pulls us from the bottom up, inspiring us to stretch and reach for the sky. As we consider layer upon layer of our personal stories through the energetic chakra system, our wounds come out of their prison of darkness and bask in multi-colored rays, receiving the deep comfort and hope-filled healing they rightfully deserve.

I offer my words with sacred intent. I trust you will hear what is meaningful for you and leave the rest. I believe we are each here by a divinely sanctioned design. May your story (all of it) be the catalyst for expressing your truest human potential. There is so much more to you! No matter where you are right now, or where you have been, keep moving. Find your way through the darkness . . . to the beauty and the integration of the rainbow light.

With sincere appreciation,

Donna DeNomme
January 17, 2014

Table of Contents

The significance of personal story seen through the chakra system
The 8 Keys to Wholeness

Muladhara chakra—red / grounding / root

Regardless of where you have been or where you are now, there is a great potential for healing. Through the Root Chakra, we discover a powerful and ever-present resource in the very earth beneath our feet. We realize that no matter what happens, we are never broken, never lost, but can navigate our way through our pain, trusting the healing force within us to know the way. We find our sure footing by embracing our sacred roots, and paradoxically, we learn to soar.

Swadhisthana chakra—orange / sexual chakra / creative chakra

In this Sacral Chakra, we recognize our ability to create, including birthing ourselves anew. Through the inspiration of an ancient myth, we see that the journey into the depths of the Underworld can hold some value, and we seek a deeper understanding of the suffering that we have endured. We examine the subtle influence of the Divine Feminine and our eternal attraction back to Her. With Her gentle, yet powerful influence, we invite the union of the feminine and the masculine within us, in order to express balance and rightful power in our lives.

Sahasrara Chakra—Crown / Violet / Divine connection with all things

The Crown Chakra beckons us to remember the essential Web of Life through which all things are connected. We recognize our interrelationship, including the harshly contrasting forms of what may appear as a seeming dichotomy of opposites. In this center, empathy for others appears, and we also move deeper into the understanding that our healing affects the entire whole. Rainbow healing emerges with strong and lasting effects, as we consider our experiences as a powerful gateway to higher consciousness and soul evolution.

The Soul Star Chakra above the head with the Earthstar Chakra below feet and the High Heart Chakra between the heart and throat—transpersonal / Soul connected / karmic / intergrative

The 8th Key to Wholeness is reflected through an empowered triad of chakras, providing a strong axis for manifesting true and lasting change. The idea of our particular soul imprint is explored, as the 8th Key moves us more fully into our transpersonal awareness. We honor our wounds, as we continue to explore their meaning and higher purpose, and as we boldly step forward in life, we elevate our expression into more of what it can be. We may even become change agents to positively affect our world. Activating our protection from the inside out, we travel full circle and ground into safety. Our experience is significant, and our lives matter.

Author's Beginning Notes:

The voice in this book is distinctly feminine. This does not mean that men cannot read this material or that it is not meant for men. Because I have grown through my experiences as a female child/adult, and because my work primarily focuses on girls and women, using feminine pronouns was the natural thing for me to do. I ask your understanding, in the same way that many of our books are written from the perspective and pronoun focus of the masculine lens.

If you are in the midst of extreme trauma, or are having great difficulty functioning in your daily life, seek out professional help. If you are in such a dark place that you are considering taking your life, contact a suicide prevention hotline or trained professional.

This book offers help and various concepts for your consideration, but it is not meant as a lifeline in times of dire need, although it will be such for some people. You are encouraged to use it in conjunction with other medical, alternative, and psychological treatment modalities. Keep yourself safe.

The 8 Keys to Wholeness Correlate with 10 of Your Chakras

Soul Star

Crown

Third Eye

Throat

High Heart

Heart

Solar Plexis

Sacrum

Root

Earthstar

Although we do not fully understand the mysterious inner phenomena of the chakras, they are imagined to be the centers for the essential life force surrounding, permeating, and emanating from within particular parts of the human body. In India this force is called prana; in China, chi; Pythagoreans called it luminous body light; and in the Middle Ages, Paracelsus spoke of illiaster, the vital force. Chakras metabolize different kinds of energy, transmitting them to appropriate places within the auric field.

~ The Book of Symbols[3]

Chakras are both a clear mirror and a powerful tool. They reflect our mental, emotional, and physical health. And by turning our conscious awareness to this naturally-occurring system, we can easily tap into its vast energy for enrichment and healing.

The Rainbow Bridge

The Significance of Personal Story Seen Through the Chakra System
The 8 Keys to Wholeness

The profound presence and lasting message of the human chakra system is ancient. Its influence has stood the test of time. By looking at our stories through this inclusive yet varied lens, we can examine our personal pain and suffering from different angles and different dimensions. As we shift the vantage point of our perspective, a fuller understanding surfaces.

At the same time, the individual chakras also provide comfort and healing for our wounds, and a protective container through which we can navigate even the most demanding personal challenge. When seen through this innately familiar chakric perspective, which we quite literally embody, both challenge and success hold innate goodness. These energy centers and the 8 Keys to Wholeness that they provide offer organization and structure for our deepest explorations—a rainbow bridge stretching from wounded to healed.

As a practitioner and teacher of conscious energy studies, I work directly with the chakra system. Even as a young girl, I could see the colors that emanated from the body; often these were guideposts that alerted me to the nature of those around me and whether or not they could be trusted. I learned to depend on my sixth sense, just as much as my other five. With a father who was gifted in this regard, my abilities were naturally accepted and nurtured. Until I formally taught classes as an adult, I never knew that this ability was unusual or that others were not working with the energy I so readily trusted. Whether you "see" energy or not, or can feel the energy coming from the location of the individual chakras, working within this structure can improve physical, mental, and emotional health.

The energies expressed through the chakras influence us intrapsychically, as seen in our inner health and balance, as well as interpersonally, as reflected in how we interact with the greater world around us. Although this book is not meant as a chakra study, we will touch on each of the major chakras with a brief summary that directly relates to our healing journey.

The chakra system is relevant not only to healing, but to the abuse itself, because abuse is, by its nature, an energetic attack having long-lasting repercussions lodged within the energetic body. In my case, the resulting marks, rips, and holes that were forcibly created in my energetic field magnetized me toward a path of healing study, partly in an attempt to relieve my fragmented self and reclaim my wholeness.

Wounds often seek a desired balance through healing. This understanding helps us to move from being stuck in the trauma onto a healing path, which ultimately results in elevated well-being. For us to remain stuck in our wounds misses the greater lesson— our stories are not just about what happened to us. Our lives are about what we did with what happened to us.

Are you wondering how healing can possibly occur with something that hurts so much? Or something that has been a part of you for so long? Don't worry about how this will all come together. Let's just move step-by-step through the chakra system as we consider it as a container for our healing—looking just in front of us, now, only as far as our head-lights allow us to see.

1st Key

Finding Our Footing
Through Sacred Roots

And the journey is an evocation of three things in particular:

a landscape that is incomparable,

a time that is gone forever,

and the human spirit, which endures.

~ N. Scott Momaday[4]

The *Muladhara* or Root Chakra grounds us in intention and purpose, connects us with the Mother (Gaia), and reconnects us with our human beginning. Through this center, we can acknowledge and appreciate our childhood through all of our growing and developing years, leading to the present. The solidity of our connection with the earth and our rootedness within her natural vibrancy supports us as we stretch upward into the task at hand, believing and knowing that we are capable of doing justice to all that we have carried for so long.

At the Root Chakra, we discover our natural connection to our own personal base, including remnants of childhood memories and their impact upon us. Whether or not your wounds originated in childhood, this chakra can help you identify and acknowledge your wounding and lead you to discover the #1 Key to Wholeness: that regardless of where you have been or what you have experienced, there is a great potential for healing by finding firm footing through your sacred roots. There is a natural healing energy that supports you and holds you up every day, and that energy is literally as close as the earth beneath your feet. The ground below you not only supports you physically by holding your body upright and holding you present via gravity, but it also supports you energetically.

The Root Chakra is located at the very base of the spine. Its powerful energy helps to ground you through your lower extremities, moving toward and into the earth. By recognizing that you are a part of a vast system that supports growth and evolution, you can tap into this remarkably resilient source for comfort, personal clearing, regeneration, and inspired growth.

Pivotal to this understanding is the recognition that we are a part of everything else in the natural world, connected to All-of-Creation. When you focus on exploring your own pain and your own imbalance, and you actively heal those wounds, your healing affects the greater collective; your personal experience impacts the rest. As you heal, you help to bring healing to our planet—and anything you can do to help bring healing to the planet ultimately helps to heal you, too. What happens to the natural world affects all of us, without discrimination, whether we are ignorant or aware of it. At the end of this first key, we will deepen with these ideas and their personal healing potential.

Right now, I ask that you imagine that you are standing with sure footing on the very ground beneath you. Now imagine that the firm and supportive ground beneath you contains precious roots to support and nourish your journey. These roots do not limit you to one place, but rather are vast and pliable. You move easily with the fluidity of your rootedness, and every step you take moves you forward toward healing. But first, you must recognize and acknowledge the very existence of the wounding.

My feet touch the cold stone as I raise myself up on the first step. Darkness looms above me, but I move on, rising onto the next step, and the next. Suddenly, above me blazes the brightness of a burning cross, angry with flames of red and gold; co-existing with the darkness that contains it; burning with an ancient message, larger than woman, fueled by man. My small hand reaches for the cold, yet beautifully ornate handle of the door. My body shakes with indescribable terror.

"Breathe," murmurs a gentle voice, "Breathe. . . ."

Louder, and laced with an anxiety that speaks with understandable concern, "You have not taken a breath for a very long time. Breathe!"

I feel a sudden burst of fresh air enter the stillness of my paralyzed body, frozen with terror, frozen in time. My breaths continue, one after the other, in little shallow puffs, in and out. It is as if there is a dense weight holding my lungs captive beneath it, my heart held tight and constrained by association.

"Where are you?" she asks.

"Church."

As an adult, I had a good life and was considered successful; I was respected by those who knew me. Although unconventional, the profession I created gracefully wove my skills into days that afforded the luxury of my wide interests. I was a guide who journeyed with others into the undiscovered jungles of their own wilderness, searching through dense emotional and psychic brush, rich with the sweet taste of new fruit. With inspired passion, I encouraged people onward as we hacked through tangled vines of limitation and wounding that tugged at weak ankles. Together we cultivated clarity and strength. We moved onward, always onward, to the certain beauty that lay ahead . . . .

Yet, ever since I had studied human development and psychology at Cornell University so many years before, I recognized that there was something not-quite-right about me. What was that? I could never really put my finger on it, but it showed itself in the subtle way that my hands never felt a part of me—not simply because I found them ugly in appearance, but because they felt detached at the wrist, almost like they had been "cut off" somehow. At other times, I had a mysterious desire to escape them, wondering if they were in fact severed, would I then feel more whole? None of this made any logical sense to me. Still, as one who was born with the fascination of what makes people who they are, I readily recognized that there was a powerful force bubbling beneath my own surface.

In the fall of 1992, I registered for a professional six-week course with Beatrice Adair, a transformational practitioner with years of experience in the field of trauma healing. I believed that this training would be a good addition to my professional practice. We were asked to fill out a questionnaire including a timeline, probing, "Where do you consider yourself on the continuum of your healing?" I inexplicably drew a huge X over and over, marring the awaiting line, noting, "I consider this course purely educational, not therapeutic." Even though my reaction seemed oddly extreme at the time, I submitted the form without remaining focused there, and proceeded on with the course.

During week three, we saw a provocative film about survivors of childhood abuse. Afterwards, during a brief silent meditation I spontaneously saw an image in my mind's eye of a very distinct form: the minutest details of a tiny acorn. I watched intently as the multi-lined top suddenly popped open, and an inky black liquid oozed out in a furious stream. The feeling of something being released washed over me, a catalyst for extreme agitation, as I was overcome with a sense of being terribly unsettled. Within the next 24 hours, the feeling grew like a sore getting worse and worse, demanding attention. I dialed Miss Bee's phone number without a clear plan, and when I heard her voice on the recorded message, a flood of tears made it almost impossible to speak. Choking through the power of my emotion, I squeaked in a little crow-like voice, "I think I need an appointment with you."

Breaking out in insuppressible sobs was highly unusual for me. Even as a child, I was one who yelled or fought but did not shed tears in response to difficulty or frustration. Obviously, I had pierced the nut! For the first time in my life, I asked for help with the unseen psychic force, the absolute terror, that had followed me since I was very young—a sense that I was NEVER, EVER SAFE. No matter where I was, no matter what I was doing, somehow they could find me. And I didn't even know who "they" were . . . .

For months, I could only reach the steps with that blazing cross blocking the threshold. For months, I could not speak about what I was seeing. Each time the terror was incomprehensible, consuming me. Yet, I must have worn down the spell of it, for eventually I was able to reach up and grasp that ornate handle in my six-year-old hand and pull with all my might, opening the massive door looming above me . . . .

Once inside, the vestibule is even more massive, and eerily still. The only sound is my cautious and quiet step upon the glistening surface of the cold, polished floor beneath me. The exquisitely detailed carvings, life-like statues, and fine furnishings are well tended; not a speck of dirt nor a crinkled paper mar the perfection of this pristine palace. I slowly creep in further. Long rows of stark oak pews with red cushions line the sanctuary. Strong cylinder pillars support the weight of the lofty vaulted ceiling above. There, in front of me, is the same looming cross that had blocked my entry. With the fire now extinguished, I see the Christ figure hanging helplessly upon it, tiny drops of blood emanating from his wounds.

A sudden movement catches my attention, as I realize with a start that there are others here. A young girl kneels on the altar steps, rigid with the unbending marble beneath her. A priest skillfully motions sacred symbols in the air above her, intent upon the ceremony in progress. The pews are empty, the room vacant of voices joined in celebratory song . . . this appears to be a sacred rite, but where is everyone else? I feel myself tense as I watch the priest grasp the layers of cloth that adorn his form and silently raise his garment. I am riveted to the scene before me as I observe the most minute detail of the eyelet lace moving slowly past my frozen eyes.

Terror strikes again with the realization that I am the one kneeling on this altar. I am the child watching the priest purposely raise his gown. Right before my widened eyes grow inexplicably dark, I feel a strong, forceful hand on the back of my head directing my child's face toward the form in front of me. The last thing I remember is my mouth being prodded open . . . . In the midst of the smell of frankincense and myrrh, I feel myself choking.

And then I am on my back as the cold, hard stone pushes unmercifully at my small, flattened body. Something is looming above, but I won't look, for it terrifies me to see it. Instead, my eyes wander to the warmth of the flame lit on the sides of the altar. From where I helplessly lie, I can see the red and the blue of the glass cradling the tiny lights with the brilliant yellow and red flames. I find comfort in the blue candles (never the red) and the contrast of the bright fiery glow of the flame, which seems to surround me and hold me in its warmth. Whatever is happening on the cold stone floor is far, far away from what I experience within those flames. I am comforted and left intact, even as my crumpled body lies dismembered on the steps leading to Jesus.

I am certain the priests have no idea that I am saved, or they would have never let me escape. They believe they capture my mind and my heart, but they only ravage my virginal outer form. They never reach the essence of the core of me.

I remember the time I took my son, Michael who was only six, to the huge Public Library in Ithaca, New York, and found myself paralyzed with sudden fear and inexplicable anxiety as I mounted the big stone steps. I became so disoriented that I barely slid down onto my bottom, as the world around me spun in a demonic whirl, threatening to cause a fall onto the cold, hard, and dark stone. "Come on, Mommy, let's go. I want to look at the books," Michael urged me onward, but I couldn't even speak. I just gazed, helplessly, at his little expectant face. He tugged on my hand, "Mommy, please. Let's go!" I stood rather shaken; although I was now able to move, psychic freedom was a thing of the past. I no longer knew when the unexpected wave of anxiety might surface, literally bringing me to my knees. Michael, a precocious child, became adept at helping me through the disorientation of my own six-year-old flashbacks whenever they surfaced. "Mom, just do one thing at a time, and then move to the next," he offered once when I was immobilized in my own kitchen, stuck within the demanding schedule of an Ivy League undergraduate student who was also the single parent of a young genius in a parent-run school for gifted children.

PTSD (Post-Traumatic Stress Disorder) is a disturbing and common occurrence for those who have experienced intense trauma. It is "a persistent re-experiencing of the traumatic event, either through intrusive thoughts, distressing dreams, through actually feeling as if the traumatic event were re-occurring in the present, or through a compulsion to repeat the trauma over and over in one's relationships."[5] Dr. Ana Mozol continues, quoting author Judith Herman as saying that "Traumatic memories lack verbal narrative; rather they are encoded in the form of vivid sensations and images."[6]

As each layer of my trauma was peeled, its existence was often forgotten because a part of me resisted its influence in my life. I now realize that long before the paralysis of anxiety that first struck in Ithaca, there were intolerable night terrors. Ironically, at the time, I was Donna Lafferty, who lived on Pleasant Street in Wellsville, New York! All was not well in Wellsville. Around three or four in the morning, I would sometimes awaken, consumed by a seemingly irrational terror. Often I would call my friend Victoria, who would talk me through it without demanding that I carry on a reasonable conversation with her. She would chat about whatever, as if it were three o'clock in the afternoon. Her husband, on the other hand, was less understanding, often wondering out loud what that crazy woman was doing calling in the middle of the night again. On the rare occasion that

I could get through one of these episodes on my own, I did so by moving with my awareness into one of the strong colors in the painting on my wall. I found the blue particularly soothing.

Even night terrors were not the very first glimmer of the underlying wound that was locked in my unconscious memory. As is often the case with what might be considered our "core" challenges, life brought me the perfect circumstance to take me deeper into issues I needed to meet and eventually master—those issues initially raised by a childhood of emotional, sexual, and religious abuse. One such pivotal time presented itself when I was abducted by a dangerous gang as a teenager:

> *My small frame rolls tightly into a ball as I bury my head into the rough cloth of my jeans, rustling this way and that with the uncontrollable vibration of my shaking legs. Huddled here on a small piece of the floor in the backseat of a '63 Chevy Impala moving at great speed, my long straight hair shields me from the light, but little more, as I quiver with intense fear in the self-imposed darkness—terrified at the reality that I cannot escape. Gunshots pierce the car's boundaries . . . .*
>
> *"I'm going to die and my mother will think I was WITH these people."*
>
> *Just a short time before, I had been standing in the warm spring sun, basking in the freedom found in a day of skipping school. I loved the Lordship luncheonette, a popular hang-out and one of my personal favorites. I spent a lot of time there, sometimes wandering peacefully along the adjacent beach. That morning, the beach was not yet populated by the droves of families who would invade this stretch in a few weeks.*
>
> *"Nothing living should ever be treated with contempt. Whatever it is that lives, a man, a tree, or a bird, should be touched gently, because the time is short."[7] Where did I first read that? It was on a plaque in a craft fair somewhere. I can't*

remember exactly where, but it struck me immediately with the ring of truth, so I scratched the poem down on a paper bag I was carrying in my backpack. Since then, I would often scroll these words with my finger stuck in the warm sand, sometimes decorating the words with shells and seaweed to create a natural altar of sorts. This one act felt more significant than anything else I did—leaving my words in the sand for who knows who to see. Today I had taken time and care in adorning my masterpiece. Walking back toward the street, I turned once more to see my work framed by strong waves crashing against the shore behind it. There was something endearing and timeless in this moment.

The luncheonette was nothin' fancy—one room with a grill behind the counter for taking orders, a few tables and chairs (inside and out), two pinball machines, a cigarette machine, and a long strand of fly paper hanging in the corner, complete with this month's gathering of flies. The smell of burgers on the grill merged with the moist salt air . . . .

While I was leaning against the front stoop minding my own business, I was approached by Vinny Giuliani,[8] a guy I kind of knew. Well, not really. I just knew him from seeing him around with my friend Tonto (Patrick De Luca). Those two had been friends since they were little kids, and their uncles were "family" connected—no one messed with them for fear of mob retaliation. Vinny had always been nice to me, so when he offhandedly mentioned, "I have an errand to run and I need a chick to assist me," I didn't even blink an eye before I agreed. Although I was an A student most of my life and considered myself fairly street-savvy, it just never crossed my mind to question the situation. Those were the days of carefree abandon, when I was seemingly immune to any great harm . . . which is how I found myself here on the floor of this freakin' car, curled up in a little ball, shaking for my life.

And that isn't the half of it. Practically as soon as we got into the car, I felt something hard poke into my ribs and looked down to see the shiny barrel of a gun in my side. "What IS GOing ON?" I screeched, digging my nails into Vinny's arm. The guy with the gun was known to be short-tempered and unpredictable, and I was wishing I was snug in my desk at school taking that Algebra test I was avoiding. It was right at that exact moment that Danny found another use for that gun when he noticed a car following us. I never was sure if it was because he feared for my safety or he just wanted more room to navigate, but in one swoop, Danny lifted me up and deposited me on the back seat. "Get down, NOW, and stay there," he shouted. "Pop, pop, pop," I heard above my head, as the car picked up speed, throwing my body this way and that as we took the corners. "Motherfuckers, take that!" Danny shouted out the window as he fired back.

Now, after what seems like an eternity of gunfire above me, I begin to pray like a frightened schoolgirl, quickly offering my deals up to God. "Get me outta here, and I won't ever skip school again . . . . I'll listen to my mother, I promise. . . . Shit, I'll even brush my teeth three times a day. Please, God, whatever it takes. I'm too young to die!"

After what feels like an eternity, the car comes to a halt and the guys get out. All I can hear is mumbling. I sit up on the backseat and straighten myself, still shaking, but now calm enough to be embarrassed about the whole cowering on the floor thing. I'm not one to normally show fear. With temporary amnesia, I'm not the least bit concerned that these yoyos basically kidnapped me at gunpoint. It's just good to be alive!

The car door swings open and with great relief I see my friend, Tonto. "Don't be afraid," he reassures me, "I won't let anything happen to you. They just want to talk to you."

"Me? What for?"

The dry wood creaks as we step onto the porch of this beachside cottage, its paint *chipping off the door jam. I watch a grey and white piece fall to the deck in slow motion . . . what are they going to do to me? Quickly glancing around, I realize there are only men in the room—except for Tonto, Vinny, and another guy, James B., I don't know any of them. They lead me through the living room into a back bedroom (without a bed, thank God). If they're gonna rape me, you'd think there'd be a bed at least.*

The room is sparse with only an old wooden desk in one corner. On top of the desk, a book lies open, with a notebook next to it and a pen in the book's spine holding its place until the reader can return. There's a pile of clothes in another corner that appear to be dirty and clean all mixed in together; at least, that's what I think at first glance. There's a sleeping bag nearby, all rolled up, and again my mind goes to the rape potential, but no one seems to be moving in that direction.

A tall guy with long brown hair and a Fu Manchu moustache motions to a solitary chair that has been spun around from that maple desk. Without a word spoken, I know from the glare of his eyes looking deeply into mine (and right through me) that my only choice is to comply. So, I sit.

What a nightmare! For several hours, I look up into the stern faces of these very scary men, circling me like wild cats stalking their prey, asking me questions that I have no answers for. My best friend, Gigi, is dating the president of their rival club, and they assume she might have told me something useful for them. Nada! I don't know what I would do if I had any information, but since I don't, all I can do is ride it out until finally the grueling interrogation ceases.

When it's over, Tonto and Vinny take me back to the beach luncheonette, reassuring me on the ride.

"You did really good. Freddy was pleased," Tonto said.

"Didn't mean to scare you," added Vinny, "Are you going to be all right?"

"Sure," I reply nonchalantly. I'm way too cool to let on that my stomach is in knots and my head is pounding. But it's over. I won't fall for something like that again.

. . . In a bit of destiny's roll of the dice, I show up at school the next day to find that my girlfriend Gigi is ignoring me completely. When the 3:15 bell rings, I hear the roar of motorcycles approaching the traffic circle out front. It doesn't take me long to realize that the rival gang is coming for me. I frantically dial the number to the payphone outside the beach luncheonette, and when James B. answers, I blurt out, "The Legends are at the high school. What should I do?"

"Stay put," he says.

When a group of thirty Harleys pulls up to the front door of Plockton High, I see the brilliance of the sun reflected off those shiny mufflers. No longer crouched in the dirt and darkness of the backseat floorboards, I'm now "rescued" by my "heroes." In typical adolescent logic, I totally forget they are the reason I am being pursued in the first place!

This was my introduction into four wild and intense years in which I explored a ripple in life's ordinary pattern. Whether I was pulling some crazy scheme with that weasel, James B.; sitting up all night with Jogo, the illustrator for Mad Magazine who would throw knives between my feet as a way to get inspired; shoving my 89-pound frame through a teeny, tiny window to get into somewhere that I wasn't supposed to be; or ruthlessly harassing members of one of our rival gangs, life was a warped kaleidoscope of chaotic adventure. Paradoxically, it was in this dangerous whirlwind that I found my firm emotional grounding and began to feel safe as I grew a thicker skin, necessary in the outlaw world in which I freely travelled. I sometimes packed a "piece" (gun) tucked in my belt next to the softness of my young belly-skin, and I always carried a knife in the inside of my left boot. Being armed in this way and with the protection of the gang, I believed no one could again take advantage of me. This lifestyle also allowed for a dramatic acting-out of the intense rage caused by what had been done to me; my explosiveness was tolerated, and in some cases, even welcomed. Having known complete powerlessness, I now fought for power over. I gained quite a reputation for being fearless, because anytime I was pinned, no matter what the size of the oppressor looming above me, I literally blacked out and severely hurt whoever was on top of me. Even though I was small in stature, I could brawl with the best of them.

Life's Unexpected Turns

Sometimes strange occurrences that initially appear "bad" can be ultimately good in the overall scheme of things, significant in helping to shape our character. Through all of our twists and turns, there is a potential for valuable lessons in our personal evolution. In retrospect, we may weave fine threads of understanding from the most surprising of life's experiences. Even though in the moment we may seem off track, in spite of their outer appearance, our detours can sometimes hold lasting value. Such was the case with this time of my life.

What could be considered a strong example of adolescent rebellion also became a significant piece of my evolutionary chain. I was able to survive in dangerous situations by drawing on a skill that I had developed during the earlier abuse—listening to my inner guidance. Finding comfort and encouragement from a group of inner spiritual guides, I learned that these unseen forces, these Beings of Light, were as real as the outer world. I came to see that these often gentle, yet powerful beings were present in the chaos to help me. Although they did not stop the abuse or change my adolescent antics, they helped me navigate *through* them. I believe I was meant to survive, and these inner guides became my healthy way out. And because of the guardian angel on my shoulder (my most outspoken inner guide) who often shouted, "Get out, NOW!" I was gratefully kept out of jail (or worse) during those teen years. But there were several treacherous close calls.

The two guys were frisked and the cops found shells, but no gun. They're taking us down to the police station so we can be properly searched. Dee is clean, but I have the gun Tonto slipped me when the cops pulled us over. It's well hidden beneath the layers of my wrinkled and baggy shirt, snug between my belly and my belt.

When we move as directed toward the back seat of the cop car, Tonto shoots me a glance. (I think he and I are soul family because whenever I am in trouble, he always miraculously shows up right when I need him. We seem to have a way of communicating without words.) His glace speaks volumes, and I immediately know what I must do.

Tonto distracts the cops with some mindless comment as I duck to get in, and in a last-ditch effort to avoid getting arrested, I slip the gun under the car. Although my hand is shaking slightly, the gun lands without an audible sound, at least nothing that can be heard above Tonto's raised voice yelling something about unwarranted police harassment.

While the cop car pulls away, I catch a gleam in the rear view mirror. There's the gun in full view, shining in the reflection of the street light, easily illuminated for all to see. Yet, by some unseen grace, only I notice it from my vantage point in the middle of the back seat.

After a couple hours of interrogation and a proper and thorough search, they let us go. Remarkably, when we return to the spot under the streetlight, the abandoned gun is still there, waiting to be reclaimed!

Times like these pointed out just how dangerous these escapades really were. I witnessed first-hand the harsh consequences of our wild endeavors: some friends were killed, several others went to prison, and still others sustained physical wounds that would impact the rest of their lives. The first time I heard gunfire after the kidnapping incident, I curiously open the door to the clubhouse and barely escaped being shot. Tonto tackled me in the nick of time.

Yet, at this point in my development, the freedom I experienced within this group afforded me the confidence I needed to "take care of business," whatever might come my way. Because my "old man" (boyfriend) was in jail, as a "little sister," I was often taken to places that I would not normally be. I was treated as a valued side-kick, given the protection of the den, and allowed to take certain liberties that were not necessarily the norm. Somewhere under my rough outer surface, a gentle healing was beginning to stir. The inclusiveness of the gang, with its clearly defined code of values, impacted the stark reality of what I had seen as the discrepancy between masculine and feminine influences in the world. Even though there were strongly different roles for the men and the women in this gang, it was clear to me that I could depend on this *tribe* of women and men to support me. I also learned to survive, to take care of myself, and to grow with an understanding of who I was in the world, separate from any assumptions or expectations of the outer, mainstream society. My resilient inner core began to emerge.

Ironically, the so-called-big-bad-outlaws forced me to finish high school and kept me away from the very worst of drugs, which were forbidden within their ethical code. Although the gang members appeared nasty and heartless to the outer society, four formative years (14-18) within this motorcycle gang held many precious and tender moments. One time my brother, Tonto, unexpectedly showed up to take me shoe shopping. He said the guys had noticed I was badly in need of shoes and in their meeting had designated club money to buy me a new pair. I was physically and emotionally cared for in many ways and found that the very best parts of their personalities were shared within the privacy of our clan.

Some people have questioned whether I, like Patty Hearst, developed a "Stockholm syndrome" connection with my abductors. Perhaps that could be true. I do admit that the experience, like life itself, was not entirely easy; and still, an understanding of simple group dynamics tells us that when one group is at odds with the dominant society, they by necessity often pull inward and direct their very best efforts toward the members of their group. As a spiritual coach, I truly believe in the synchronicity of our life experiences, and this particular one filled a gaping emotional hole left within me. My being so young and impressionable allowed this "ruthless" gang to play an important role by finishing the job of raising me. I gleaned an important ethical perspective that continues to guide me today: a central code of brotherhood and undying loyalty, an understanding of how to take care of someone else, and even more importantly, a knowing of how to allow someone else to "watch my back." I also found healing in a tribal setting, escaping the constraints of being a ritually-abused, distrustful victim because of the personal empowerment discovered during this pivotal time.

Trusting the Healing Force within You

Within you there is a natural and creative force pushing toward healing and growth; where it bubbles up cannot be predicted. This inner force helped me to grow beyond a survivor into someone much more personally empowered. In later years, my foremost teaching became one of encouraging others to embrace a path of healing, rather than allowing themselves to stay stuck in a destructive patterns that continued to wound, perpetuating a victim role.

There is an inner evolutionary drive that seeks to find balance. Open to what is within you that *knows* there is more, regardless of the challenge of where you have been or where you are right now. And try not to harbor harsh, rigid judgments about what is life's most fruitful path. Often it is that which hurts us which, ultimately, shapes our character. Our greatest gifts may be wrapped up in seemingly insurmountable challenges. The Sufi poet Rumi offers this understanding:

This being human is a guesthouse
every morning a new arrival.

A joy, a depression, a meanness,
some momentary awareness comes
as an unexpected visitor.

Welcome and entertain them all!
Even if they're a crowd of sorrows
who violently sweep your house empty of its furniture.
Still, treat each guest honorably.
He may be clearing you out
for some new delight.

The dark thought, the shame, the malice.
Meet them at the door and invite them in.

Be grateful for whatever comes.
Because each has been sent
as a guide from beyond.[9]

Never Broken, Never Lost

You cannot judge something by how it looks on the outside. In the religiously-oriented, trusted school and church community where I was supposed to be taken care of and mentored in my spiritual development, I was raped and brutally terrorized—and in a violent outlaw society, I found safe haven, the nurturing of a clan, and healing for my battered psyche.

We also cannot judge others for their experience, or ultimately know what that experience will mean to them. Even when it appears that others have been broken by trauma or lost to life's hardships or abuse, that may not be the truth for them—we cannot judge their lessons or ways of developing. People and situations must stand on their own merit, not on how others see them. Character is much more than skin deep. I have witnessed unexpected potential within academically challenged, special needs children, mentally and emotionally unstable adults, and incarcerated women felons. Sometimes in the darkest room you can find the brightest light.

Know that whatever has happened to you or is happening to you, it is only a part of who you are. Do not let it dictate your direction or limit your possibilities. No one or nothing can define you—unless you allow it to hold you captive. The Ultimate Truth moves from the inside out, as personal insight integrates into purposeful action. In assessing and opening to the deeper meaning of each part, we release hidden potential. This is *your* life!

In a topsy-turvy, pliable world, life's pendulum swings, and life comes together in remarkable ways. At times, it is through the contrast of others that we find our truest selves. Up against the ominous authority of the priests and the Catholic Church as a whole, there was no place left for me to stand, as a (female) child, except in their shadow. This afforded the selection of a different path: a shamanic, healing, and spiritual one—a path fed by resources and teaching outside of the constraints of a rigid religious system. I learned to accept the perfection of life unfolding and the inner guidance to direct it.

This understanding developed a trust that led me in very unconventional directions. Over a period of three decades, I found myself drawn to indigenous healers and teachers and was given a way to make sense of even the most bizarre childhood occurrences. Shamanism provided a brilliant container for the dark, penetrating wound that had stolen my innocence. It also provided *grounding* for my soul's path of redemption.

The Muladhara Chakra: finding our roots

Like a tree, we can only reach as high as our roots grow deep and wide, needing the stability of the earth to support our lofty spiritual flights. Being energetically grounded in the density of the earthly soil allows us to stretch beyond the limits of our human containers. And through our earthly connection, we are offered resources outside of us, paradoxically helping us to tap the vast potential within. I recognize that the natural world—Mother Earth and Father Sky; mountains, valleys, and bodies of water; trees, birds, and even the tiniest creepy-crawlies—have supported me in more ways than I can ever convey.

I have come to the mountain to sit in meditation, prayer, and song for three days. At times, I even engage in a little dance inside my tiny circle, the circumference of which is equal to my height. This is a sacred circle of clear intention, seasoned with offerings and a humble request of the natural world and the powers-that-be, asking for a sign of guidance. After I sit for a very long time, as is the course for this solitary Hemblecha (Native American Vision Quest), I receive a treasured gift. In the last few minutes before I'm released from the expansive limits of what appears to be a small, contained circle, the earth opens to receive me as her daughter.

I watch as a small crack in the dirt beneath me grows in girth, until it opens with an invitation to crawl inside. I easily move within her womb and am cradled in the warm earth as she surrounds me. I feel her primal embrace. I feel her love and support. I speak words of alliance, dedicating myself as a conscious Earth Guardian; no longer will I keep still when I see others harming her. In my own small way, I will support her desperate need to heal. As she holds me within the depth and breadth of her scope, I know I will never be alone; Great Mother supports me from below.

Unearthing Deeper Meaning

The earth itself, as dark and fertile soil, is feminine in nature. This idea is reminiscent of the Gnostic myth of Sophia, a personification of the Wisdom of God. In the process of creation, Sophia, the divine wisdom, descended into matter, and in the course of that descent became lost and imprisoned in matter—thus becoming the hidden God in need of release and redemption. In *Sophia: The Feminine Face of God*, Karen Speerstra states that every time someone creates something, Sophia is present because her nature is creative:

> She IS you, and she's me and she's all those other beautiful women—and men— around us. She offers a deep, dark, fertile place within each of us with which to create and affirm life.[10]

Your *greatest* creation is your own life. Like the earth, you have cycles of birth and death, creating anew from the decaying soil of your past experiences. You have the opportunity to grow through the choices you make; with each new day, you cultivate your own rich soil.

As a part of recognizing our personal connection to the greater whole, many native traditions instruct the necessary return to caring for the earth as an essential path to human survival. Instead of the modern practice of stripping the earth naked, raping her precious natural resources, we must stray from the Path of Mind, a masculine-energetic that sacrifices the good of the whole for the desires of a few, and return to the Path of Heart, a feminine-energetic that values the rights of all things. *Mitakuye Oyasin*, the Lakota say, acknowledging that "all my relations" signifies a familial bond with all of life. This inclusive and diverse acceptance is a way to re-pattern our collective behavior, in order to embrace the earth with the respect she so deserves. The forgiving nature of Mother Earth is readily available to us, in spite of all that has been done to disregard her. We just need to demonstrate that we care about her and about future generations.

In September 2010, I found myself in a large circle of over 150 people who had come together to experience an earth healing ritual led by Don Oscar Miro-Quesada. My interest in this gathering arose from a simple desire to contribute in a positive energetic way to our planet. Ironically, because of one of the worst fires in Boulder, Colorado's history, our meeting was moved from its beautiful mountain setting to a hotel ballroom in town. As I left my house that morning, I noticed an unwarranted annoyance, for no apparent reason, and if it weren't for a close friend who was expecting me, I probably would have stayed home. At the same time, my inner guidance had begun to rumble, sending me a sense of the power of the day.

Joseph Campbell describes the shamanic figure as an "interpreter and intermediary between man and the powers behind the veil of nature."[11] Don Oscar, a respected Peruvian *kamasqa curandero* (a shaman),[12] was in Colorado to lead us in piercing the veil of seeming separation between the human and non-human elements and to help us to reconnect with the feminine nature of our earth.

The central altar is already set when we enter the room, and being keepers of the Pachakuti Mesa tradition, the center space is quite elaborate with mini-altars in each direction. I have not worked with Oscar before and only once shared in a ritual facilitated by one of his students. I am unknown to him.

During the initial setting of the energies, the shaman chooses the youngest person in the room (a small boy), a maiden (a young, unmarried woman), and later a crone (an older woman) to help with the ceremony. He then lowers his head in complete attention as he plays with a few objects purposefully placed in the center of our large circle. I can't see past him, but he must have thrown something down, because a metallic stone rolls over from some 20 feet away and hits my foot quite hard, spins past me, and lands in the aisle. When I look up, Don Oscar's face is peering at me from between his legs.

"Did that HIT you?"

"Yes."

"Well, PICK it UP!" he says, a bit agitated and at the same time somewhat amused. This magnetic hematite stone's touch is the sign he asked for, so Don Oscar welcomes me into the inner circle, embraces me, and asks me to hold the anchor for the west (directional) during the day-long ritual, sitting at the mesa (altar) of one of his most advanced apprentices. I am familiar with shamanic tests—honored methods of selection, which contain a connection to the spirit realm and a request for help to determine who can serve a specific role within a ceremony. During that particular morning, my own inner guidance repeatedly said, "Be ready. You will be asked to do something." My logical self argued that this was impossible; the room was filled with many long-time students of this tradition, and the ways of this particular circle were unknown to me. Still the voice clearly persisted with its consistent foreshadowing.

There's a time when Don Oscar readies me for the task to come. He clears my energetic field by cleansing my body, front and back, using sacred, scented water blown over the surface of my entire form, starting with the center of my face and moving downward. I can report that although the shaman literally spits sacred water from his mouth into my face (and the strong perfumed scent of the water remains around me for days), I find this technique in no way threatening or disruptive. Instead, it catapults me into a deep, altered inner space.

I spontaneously return to an earlier time of being raped when I was six years old. There's no trauma in this inner recollection, but instead a deep sense of peace. I am aware, in this present moment, that the rape pierced my innocence; that it was a male domination and also a wounding of the greater feminine; and that in the actual time frame, as a six-year-old, my psyche was strengthened, as was my connection with my own inner guidance. The harsh trauma actually provided the space to deepen my inner strength as a matter of physical and psychological survival. Like Alice in Wonderland, I fell down the rabbit hole into another reality at an early age and learned my way around a strange and different world just as real as this one—a remarkable world living right inside of me.

In the Peruvian tradition, there is a two-thousand-year-old prophecy that speaks of the coming of a new time. We have been in the midst of a modern, technological age, governed by the intellect at the expense of the heart, and by material prosperity at the expense of spiritual depth. The present era is represented by the eagle, which has driven out the condor. Indigenous people with a more direct spiritual connection to nature and a more heart-centered way of caring for the earth are often represented by the condor. One of the most threatened and endangered birds in the world, the condor, like the indigenous ways it represents, is in danger of disappearing. Yet, according to this prophecy, we are at the beginning of the Fifth Pachakuti—a time when the condor will rise again to once more join the eagle in the same sky, as the world returns to its lost balance.

This evolution as it relates to our healing process, individually and collectively, will be explored further as we travel through the 8 Keys to Wholeness, which evoke the balance of the masculine and feminine energies and the interrelationship of the Path of the Mind and the Path of the Heart.

Magical Flight: a shamanic portal

As Don Oscar moves to my back and continues to clear my physical form, he brushes the air around my body with two large feathers, one eagle and one condor, and continues to spray sacred water from his mouth onto my physical and etheric form.

Still in a deep, altered state, I remember a bird that took me to fly over the mountains during those years of sexual and ritual abuse. Having been raised on the East Coast, I was later drawn to, and settled in the unknown yet familiar foothills of the Rocky Mountains. Their distinct presence is the same one I remember providing psychic safety for me as a child.

In this particular ceremony, it is a distinctly different bird that I see in my mind's eye: a red-tailed hawk, clearly hovering in full detail in front of me. The minute contour of every feather is vividly accessible, the softness of her feathers so very comforting. In one heightened moment, the bird shifts from being in front of me to being all around and then through me. I become the bird.

Nature speaks through its various expressions. Birds are a strong symbol, often seen as messengers of Spirit. When I consider this particular bird, it leads me to an understanding of embracing both the strength of the wings around me, clearly felt as me, and the ability to "take flight" combined with the skill to see a great span of earth at a "bird's eye view."

One aspect of the intuitive feminine influence is our ability to move beyond the physical reality, and to experience information not usually interpreted by the five core senses. We all have this capacity, but the awareness of these subtle energies may not always be available to us. Our ability to consciously sense these pneumatic waves may be influenced by just how energetically clear we are. In this ceremony, Don Oscar cleared my physical and energetic form to make me ready. We can, on a daily basis, enhance our abilities to be open to the multi-dimensional information all around us by clearing ourselves through meditation and other centering practices, and by monitoring and neutralizing our thoughts, words, and actions.

Don Oscar spoke of recognizing a seasoned channel within me that was being called upon to "bring back the feminine for the healing of the planet."[13] He was unaware of my background or my work, both of which directly relate to his observation. At a pivotal point during this day-long ritual, my physical body was used as a conduit for healing energies coming into our sacred circle. These energies would contribute to helping restore our lost natural balance: the sacred marriage of the Mother Earth with the Father Sky.

This remarkable experience was one of many over a period of 40 years, as shamanism from Mayan, Peruvian, and Native American lineages provided me with a living core. As I explored honored traditions that were new to me, there was a familiarity, a feeling of coming home—reminiscent of times of safety as a young girl finding solace in the candle flame or in the softness of my spirit bird's wings. These ancient and highly valuable practices offer valuable guideposts for enhanced spirituality and naturally aligned living.

1st Key to Wholeness: finding our footing through sacred roots

The Root chakra is an important place to begin healing. This is the center that helps build the foundation for our journey in a way which is strong and grounded. The base chakra is often where we have stored fear created by past and present events. At times, our fear is shielded by a layer or layers of protective anger. Lashing out at others can be evidence of a deeper wound with a protective layer guarding us against further harm. Unfortunately, the very attention and love the wound needs to heal can be pushed away by the emotional protection defending it.

Now is the time to tap into the great key held in this first power center and use it to unlock further understanding about who you are and what you need. Buy a new notebook or journal, and record your thoughts as you read this book. Selecting a special notebook or a journal just for this purpose is symbolic of a fresh start, a new beginning. It's not important that you write in essay form—you can jot notes using phrases, lists, or complete sentences. Your writing does not have to make sense to anyone else; its purpose is to assist and serve you as you move through our exploration of the chakras and their 8 keys.

You may find that you don't even need to reread what you write, but that the simple act of writing invites a deeper understanding to rise into your consciousness. Opening your own channel to the inner realm can have remarkable healing capacity. In our busy lives, we often do not make time to listen to our deepest thoughts and feelings, and they may be vying for your attention.

I suggest you pause after this chapter and explore what is readily present, opening the door for more to surface. You may be well aware of the wounding you sustained. Or perhaps you long ago buried what hurt you, turning away from its strained face. Record what comes to mind by observing your thoughts. Then record what comes to heart by recording your feelings, even if there is not a thought connected to them. The more *information* you record (without judgement), the better it will be for what follows. Be sure to be gentle with what surfaces, so your innermost parts learn that it is safe to come forward. Let's cradle your most tender spots, so they can open to deep and lasting healing.

Draw in support during your exploration by engaging the help of a close friend, perhaps someone who has already done his or her work in a similar way. If you don't know someone who can mentor you through this time, I highly recommend that you seek out a qualified and compassionate counselor or coach to monitor you as you move through your own dark wilderness. An outer touchstone can be invaluable to help ease the difficulty of your navigation and to help keep you grounded on your path. Professionals do not necessarily give you answers; they are qualified guides who can help you find your *own* meaning and direction. It is a great honor for me to walk with you into your deepest, darkest forest, with the potential for carrying great understanding and wisdom into the dawning light.

Consider:
- What do you fear? Are you aware of your fears, or are they buried deep within you?
- When do fears arise? Who or what are the triggers for your fears?
- What brings up anger within you? What people or situations trigger your anger?
- What have been the challenges of your life? Take time recording these. You may want to explore each one a bit before you move on.
- What still seems raw? Unresolved? Are there difficulties that still have a hold on you and influence your life? In what ways are you still a victim? By simply acknowledging these wounds, you honor them. This is the initial step to healing.

Physical Grounding

We store our wounds in the physical containers of our bodies. I often see clients who no longer *think* about their wounding, but who exhibit physical imbalance or disease that expresses their unresolved wound. Physical pain can also be a way to avoid facing our emotional wounding. Another possibility is that some of us are not grounded in our bodies at all, but instead may emotionally "check out" of the body, actually ignoring the warning signs of our pain. The practice of leaving the body because of the intense pain found in it is often learned as a survival mechanism by those who have been traumatized. If you don't feel fully present physically, I encourage you to further explore the content of your painful roots, in order to see exactly what it is you may be trying to escape. What may have been much too big to face in an earlier time can often be quite manageable from the perspective of where you have now grown.

- What are your physical imbalances? What are your chronic ailments, aches and pains, and sensitivities? In these outer symptoms are guideposts for what is crying out with a desire to be healed.

- Are you present in your body? It is amazing how many people are not even "home!"

- Experiencing pain in your body, and dealing with the repercussions of those pains, may be one way to avoid dealing with the deeper layers of what is wounded in you. How much of your time is spent monitoring and managing pain, imbalance, or disease? How much of your week is taken up with doctor visits or physical therapy appointments?

- Set aside some contemplation time to observe what is going on with your body. Notice what you do, how you act, and how you feel—your outer reflection provides valuable information about your inner process.

Through first *being present*, and secondly *acknowledging* what is, we can then move to being open to deeper insight, understanding, and meaning. Often these things are pushed away because they are unpleasant. After being ignored for who knows how long, it may take some time to cultivate trust, in order for your innermost feelings to surface. Cultivate an environment of safety—one that welcomes all parts of you to express. You can approach this as if you were playing hide and seek with your most authentic self!

- Notice what people and what situations you most resonate with.
- Notice what people and what situations you are most repelled by.
- Sometimes it is through the *contrast* of the outer world that our understanding of our truest selves develops.

It is important to explore (and perhaps to write or talk about) how you feel about being in this world. Opening your eyes wider to your personal reality may initially stir things up, bringing uncomfortable and even painful feelings to the surface; the process of building or rebuilding is not necessarily easy or pleasant. By being honest about what you see and how you feel, you create a clear starting place, enabling you to find sure footing to move forward.

- Are you pleased to be alive?
- Do you feel that life is welcoming? Or a struggle?
- Are you braced for what will come at you next?
- Do you trust life?
- Do you think you are supposed to be here?
- Do you have a right to be in this world? Are you able to explore who and what you are by knowing that you matter?
- How do you think you contribute to your family? Your community? The greater world?
- What do you hope for?

In some way and for some reason, you are supposed to be here. You have a right to be in this world, and there is something (or many things) that you have to contribute to the whole. Never underestimate even the smallest thread in the totality of the Web of Life. Your thread affects the rest of us, and I care about whether you are seen or unseen, strong or weak, healthy or unwell.

Know that your present and your past are only a small part of who you are. They can make you weaker or stronger—the choice is yours. Let all of your experiences be recognized for the *parts* they play; no one thing becomes the single defining piece. The multi-faceted essence of who you are rises from within you, longing for its rightful expression. Listen to your own Inner Call. And remember that all things can be healed. As we go to the root, we know and declare that our foundation is not weak, but instead quite strong. We draw on support from within and from all around us, knowing that we are not alone.

> People usually consider walking on water or in thin air a miracle.
> But I think the real miracle is not to walk either on water or in thin air,
> but to walk on earth.
> ~ Thich Nhat Hahn[14]

Imagine a strong chord of brilliant red light moving from the base of your spine, the coccyx, down through both legs, and into the earth. Breathe slowly, in and out, for three or four breath cycles. Then, speak with a strong, yet gentle voice the following statement to invite activation and to embrace the support of this significant healing center:

The Root Chakra grounds my intention while connecting me with the earth (Gaia) and reconnecting me with my childhood, my teen years, and all the other years that have passed by. With a slow, easy breath, I focus on the natural connection with what is beneath me, moving with the root energy through the base of my spine, down through my legs, my shins, my ankles, and the soles of my feet.

My solid yet flexible coccyx bone, the base of my spine, allows me to stretch upward into the task at hand, believing and knowing that I am capable of doing justice to all that I have carried for so long. Centering and grounding with the energies below (the Divine Feminine), and flexing and reaching with the energies above (the Divine Masculine), gives me the strength for all that I need to meet and experience this day.

I am never alone, but rather interconnected with All-There-Is through my inherent tie to the earth and every part of the natural world. Wherever I am and whatever I am doing, in a breath, I can be in touch with the Mother below me and the Mother within me.

2ⁿᵈ Key

Returning to the Mother and Birthing Ourselves

Spirit of comfort and longing,
enfold my fear,
unclothe me of my pride,
unweave my thoughts,
uncomplicate my heart,
and give me surrender:
that I may tell my wounds,
lay down my work, and greet the dark.

~ Janet Morley[15]

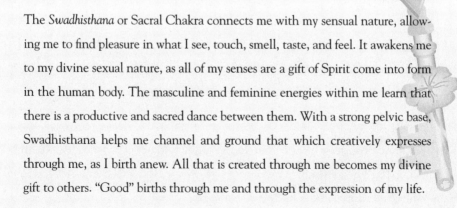

The *Swadhisthana* or Sacral Chakra connects me with my sensual nature, allowing me to find pleasure in what I see, touch, smell, taste, and feel. It awakens me to my divine sexual nature, as all of my senses are a gift of Spirit come into form in the human body. The masculine and feminine energies within me learn that there is a productive and sacred dance between them. With a strong pelvic base, Swadhisthana helps me channel and ground that which creatively expresses through me, as I birth anew. All that is created through me becomes my divine gift to others. "Good" births through me and through the expression of my life.

The 2nd Key to Wholeness helps us to discover or acknowledge the Divine Feminine and to recognize and balance the masculine and feminine energies that express through us. When we tap the multi-dimensional energies of the pelvic chakra, we are encouraged to incorporate these contrasting, yet potentially collaborative, characteristics into our lives. We learn to celebrate both the inspired and creative feminine and the practical and productive masculine; together, they can accomplish great things! In addition, the solid structure of our pelvic girdle partners with its own flexibility, providing the perfect portal for birthing anew. As we discover (or rediscover) the Great Mother, she helps us to face and heal our wounds. Within the basin-shaped physical structure of the bones connecting and supporting our trunk and legs, we also find the intestines, which provide the ability to energetically digest our emotional content, as well as physically process our daily food. The Divine Feminine innately understands the cycles of life and can show us the way to release what we have mistakenly held undigested—the emotional weight of that which does not serve us is quite a burden to bear.

In Key #1, we connected with the Earth, Gaia, Creator and Sustainer of the natural world. As we move into this second chakra, I would like to share an ancient feminine myth. You may already be familiar with this story because, gratefully, the old myths are finding their way back to us. They are being retold in small circles and large halls; they are being shared with women and men through the written word and the oral tradition. Feminine wisdom is surely resurfacing! Whether this is a new story or one you hold dear, I ask that you consider my telling of Persephone and Demeter. This story and its timeless message will soothe the way for the stark personal reality I later disclose, providing a healing salve to protect tender skin from the harshness of what follows.

I am grateful to the ancient wisdom that comes through time to create powerful containers and potent lenses through which we can find meaning in times of chaos and modern crazy-making. Life provides many opportunites for growth, wrapped in the clever disguise of comonplace difficulties and outrageous challenge.

Once upon a time, there was a girl—a sweet and delightful girl, pure as the new day. Kore was a beloved child, cherished by her doting and attentive mother, Demeter. The pair lived a good life enjoying the bounty of the natural world, as Demeter was the goddess of the grain, the harvest, and all that grew to feed the people.

One day Kore was romping carefree in the vast and abundant field, picking flowers with several of her young friends. Her sweet voice stretched far and wide, joyfully singing a tender melody. The young girl bent to pick a narcissus that bloomed next to a large black stone. When she tugged at the flower, her milky-white hand brushed the dark stone, and suddenly the earth beneath her shook. Startled, Kore dropped her basket, and the radiant spectrum—flowers of red, orange, yellow, green, indigo, and violet—spilled from their hoop. It was as if the hopeful rainbow had fallen from the sky.

Within seconds, the earth opened, and up from below rose a great chariot: dark, yet regal, with an elaborately scrolled golden bed pulled by six sturdy black steeds. The driver reached down toward Kore and as the chariot sped past, he easily lifted her inside. A loud, piercing scream cut through the warmth of the sun, leaving a chill for all who crossed its path. Unfortunately, the young girl's companions had wandered elsewhere, being now too far to hear her desperate cry. Only one, the old woman Hecaté, heard her call out to Father Zeus, the good and almighty, the Governor of All. Hecaté hurried from her cave, but she could see nothing—the girl had vanished.

For nine days and nights, Demeter sought her daughter. Eventually she was told of a crack that had opened in the earth and swallowed some swine. The swine herder had caught a glimpse of a faceless chariot driver with a shrieking young girl clasped under his arm. Demeter and Hecaté confronted Helios, the Sun, who saw everything from his vantage point high in the sky, and he reluctantly admitted that Hades, the King of the Underworld, was the kidnapper. Hades' brother was Zeus, the King of the Gods, and nothing happened in the king's kingdom that he was unaware of; so some have wondered if, in fact, Hades was acting with Zeus' blessing on a desire to take Kore as his wife.

The Greek gods and goddesses sometimes had family lineages that seem unacceptable today. Such was the case with Zeus, who was a brother not only to Hades, but also to Demeter, and father to Kore. Yet, he seemed to be deaf to the young girl's agonizing cries for help and also ignored Demeter's grief at the loss of her innocent child.

Mother Demeter roamed the earth, forbidding the natural world to grow. This being her jurisdiction, the flowers and the herbs, the grains, and all the growing fields dried up and died. The people had nothing to eat. They also had nothing to offer in sacrifice to the gods. Demeter had the attention of Zeus now! He sent Hermes to Hades with a message to return the girl rightfully to her mother. And he sent Demeter a message saying that Kore would be returned under one condition—that she had not eaten in the Underworld, that she had not tasted the food of the dead.

In the meantime, Hades offered Kore a respected place on the throne next to him, reigning over the vast kingdom of the Underworld. He also offered her a pomegranate from which she ate seven seeds, thereby linking herself to the Underworld forever. Demeter was outraged to learn that her daughter had been tricked by Hades. She planned on continuing her devastation of all that grew upon the earth; there would be nothing that any of the gods or goddesses could do to intercede upon this mother's wrath.

Zeus asked Rhea, the mother of Hades, Demeter, and himself, for sage advice. It was decided that Kore would remain with Hades for three months each year as Persephone, Queen of the Underworld. During that time, Demeter would turn her attention to grief, leaving the earth in a time of rest, and the fields and the trees would lay barren of grain or fruit. In the spring, when Persephone returned to her mother, the natural world would awaken and become fertile again. Persephone's journey, with its descent and ascent and descent again, is reflected in our seasonal changes. This ancient story also describes our personal movement from the conscious, daytime world into the less-seen and the less-known (unconscious) parts of ourselves—the places to which we go each night in our deepest dreams. Through these nocturnal journeys, we glimpse our own Underworld.

Peeking Into Consciousness

I was aware of terrifying memories of childhood abuse for most of my adult life. Yet, even before the fullness of those memories surfaced, I had reoccurring, haunting dreams with the same themes— of being chased with no one around to help me, or of being physically and sexually hurt and unable to scream, so the nearby people, who I could readily see, could notice what was happening to me. I often awoke struggling to find my voice and fighting to make a sound. Like Persephone, I had a desperate sense of being alone; no matter how many people were around me, no one could help me. The worst of the repetitive dreams depicted a variety of scenes with the same underlying dilemma.

I am warm and cozy in a luxurious bubble bath, restfully soaking my tired body. My head rests upon the edge of an old-fashioned, claw-footed tub; the coolness of the porcelain surface supports my neck, as bubbles dance across my heart, tickling my skin. I am peaceful and content.

Suddenly I sit upright in the bath, my eyes jutting wide open with shock and dismay.

"Oh, NO!" I shout inside my own head, my lips pressed tightly together as if afraid to let the horrible truth escape.

I suddenly remember that I killed someone and somehow blocked out the memory of it. In this moment, I know that I will never, ever forget again. And now that I know, even if no one else ever finds out, how can I possibly go on living my life? Now that I know that I did this horrible thing, how can I possibly live with myself?

Each time I had one of these dreams, the content was unbearable. The heaviness of the dreams filtered into my daily life, contributing to that growing feeling that something was not right with me. When the memories did surface, they came fast and furious. Their disturbing nature caused me to initially challenge them—how in the world could these shocking things be true? Where were my parents and the others when this was happening? And why didn't anyone help me? Typical to the classic pattern for abuse victims, I looked to myself for accountability and blame. Why in the world were these ideas running through my mind? And if they were true, why didn't I do something to stop the abuse when it was happening?

During this time of questioning, once again, life brought to me the perfect answers. When we are on a path of healing, life's circumstances provide exactly what we need to facilitate that healing. I worked with many clients as a licensed spiritual coach and yet, never before had I seen the types of clients that came during this time. Within a couple of short months, I had a steady stream of five new clients, ALL of whom told me the same story—that of sexual and ritual abuse within the Catholic Church. Some of their stories were even more gruesome than mine. These people had been raised in different parts of the country with similar treatment in different parishes and schools.

I sat and listened to their disclosure in our initial session and immediately, at the culmination of the hour, referred them to another professional, convinced that at this point in my own healing I was not the best one to assist them with theirs. I remained silent, never sharing my own demons. Yet, at the close of the session with my fifth client, I raised my eyes to the heavens and declared, "OK. I GET it! Don't send me these people anymore." In the outer reflection of hearing about others' wounding, I recognized that I needed to accept my own. I wholeheartedly set about the work of healing myself.

Why was I a "Victim?"

People who abuse children often select an easy mark and cultivate a relationship with a social outcast or shy kid, making them think they're special. On the contrary, I was an outgoing, popular, straight-A student. I sometimes wonder why I was chosen. As a child,

I had a lot of spunk—there is one picture of me with Santa when I was three or four years old, and I am obviously talking with great conviction. Honestly, Santa looks scared. I could be a lot to handle! So, why was I targeted?

I also wonder why I never told anyone what was going on. I was certainly outspoken. But there was no way I could tell my father, because he would kill the priest, and then he would go to jail. Years later when I did tell my Dad, his words confirmed my suspicions. I wouldn't have told my mother because she was a devout Catholic, and like the rest of my extended family thought the priests could do no wrong. Priests were messengers of God. The priest's word would always be believed over mine—his word was gospel.

I do remember one time when I threatened to tell. I was not being touched or hurt, but instead having an intense conversation in an open hallway in my grade school.

> *Even though no one else is around, I am not afraid. My classroom is only steps away, and I can see the light through the window in the closed door. I know I can reach the portal in just seconds if need be. In a more and more heated conversation with a visiting bishop, I actually blurt out that I'm going to tell people what is happening here. He lunges at me, wrapping his hands around my throat, gripping with strength and conviction.*
>
> *"I will KILL you," he croaks.*
>
> *"Go ahead," I say defiantly.*
>
> *He squeezes tighter as his eyes pierce through me, eyes glowing red with rage.*
>
> *"I am going to take your SOUL!"*
>
> *Terror moves through me. Still my natural inclination is to fight him.*
>
> *"Don't fight. That's when they get you," my inner spiritual guides firmly say.*
>
> *I stand very still without struggling. In the path of that evil glare, in a terrifying grip that threatens to choke off my very life breath, I quietly stand my ground.*

I take little shallow breaths so he doesn't know I'm continuing to breathe, continuing to live.

Finally, he releases his hold on me.

I don't necessarily believe in the devil, but it seemed that I saw the devil *that day*. My silence was bought, not because of the fear of losing my own life, and not because of the fear of losing my own soul, but because of something more typically basic. The priest guaranteed my silence by threatening to kill my little sister, who was a shy and withdrawn child, frail in many ways. Knowing first-hand what these people were capable of, I had to protect her.

Like Hades, who had the backing of the all-powerful Zeus, priests were sanctioned by the Catholic Church, which was all-mighty and powerful in my family and community. I knew there was no one to help me in the physical realm. And even though I continued to be a seemingly outgoing child, after this incident, certain things were never spoken about and rarely even considered. Yet, the body continues to hold the memory, and regardless of time's passing, the unspoken finds expression. During the writing of this book, long, thin, angry red marks appeared and rose up on my neck—they looked eerily like those fingers on the base of my throat.

In discussing what is described as "narcissistic relationships," the Rev. Thomas P. Doyle, a Catholic dominican priest and one of the world's most foremost and outspoken authorities on perpetrator priests, exposes them as those who "seldom [grasp] the devastation" their actions have caused, instead convincing the victims that "the sexual activity was special, even divinely approved."[16] The Catholic Church has often stood by those who take advantage of their children. Just like Zeus who stood by the abductor, Hades, rather than protecting Persephone, Pope John Paul II, in 1993 amidst allegations of pedophile priests, chose to respond by saying, "Yes, dear brothers, America needs much prayer, lest it lose its soul."[17] Mention of care for the victims of those priests was absent. One must wonder if, in a hierarchical organization where the Pope is at the very top of the church, the emotional and sexual abuse was, in fact, breaking news to the pontiff. Or, like the mythic Zeus did he also have prior knowledge and a larger part in "blessing" or at least condoning the acts? Bishops were often called upon to discipline the priests, and yet my clearest memory, described above, is of a visiting bishop who was the perpetrator of one of my gravest psychic abuses. Other memories, like the one below, were of more than one perpetrator, some of whom were dressed in hierarchical garb.

True Terror: the tainted host

Several of us cower in this small, cave-like room beneath the earth, below the school. Although it is a part of the basement, it feels like a crypt of sorts . . . a place for the dead . . . and for the living to visit the land of the dead. We tread into the dark abyss that is waiting to ensnare us. This is the most gruesome of days—a part of the sacred holy days of Lent before Easter. Voices rise in a mesmerizing chant that draws me with its captivating repetition, and simultaneously repels me, as its sacrilegious sound burns my ears with discordant tones.

A sacred instrument of God with the power to bless us on Sunday, the priest hovers over something wriggling with life. I see the image of complete innocence struggling beneath what can only be described as the grip of evil. His intent is known to me even beore the sight of it forever scorches my eyes. In this room beneath the earth, I feel a merciless dampness that moves through me with a shudder, as I see the priest's face contort as if he is straining under the sheer weight of his task. He performs a tainted and warped ritual sacrifice.

Deafening sounds continue in high chants, pounding at my head from all sides. I am beyond tears, frozen with a reality that short-circuits my brain, changing forever how I look at the world. My silent scream draws no savior. Sweet Jesus, how could you let this happen?

Black-robed nuns with blank faces and smiling priests receive hosts from a blessed chalice; the body of Christ / the blood of Christ spills upon the sacred white cloth. Children make their way forward as they, too, receive the little corrupt circles, blessed in this absolutely-wrong-rite that strains reason. As I find myself at hell's doorway, my spiritual leader beckons me to cross its cruel threshold.

"NO!"

I will not accept this communion. I will not be a part of this.

"No, no, a thousand times no."

I shake my head from side to side, unable to find the voice to speak the words that repeat over and over in my head: "No, no, no."

Strong hands tighten around my arms, holding me unnecessarily in the frozen state that has already paralyzed me. Any path of escape is blocked, and as I look from blank face to scowling face, I know without a glimmer of hope that in the darkness of these shadows, there is nowhere to go. Still my mind says, "No. I will not take that thing into my mouth. This cannot be right. You are not right. Never again will I believe you and your lies about God."

"God help me," I cry silently with all my might. "Please, God, help me."

No one hears. No one comes. Held on either side, I struggle no more, until the shiny gold of the rich chalice is held in front of my eyes, and the deceiving purity of a lily-white host is raised high into the air. "No, I will not!" I grip my mouth shut and struggle right and left, right and left, right and left, thrashing my head and neck as much as possible within the human vice that holds my young body. I fall backwards as I'm dropped to the floor. More hands tightened around my head as the corrupt communion pushes tirelessly against my lips.

"NO!" I hold my lips taut as he continues to push, cruel eyes demanding my compliance. Those eyes burn a hole through my forehead. I strain not to look at

them directly, as I fear they will cause me to disappear altogether. His is a force
that has the ability to steal life.

Sweat drips on my face and my hair as the priest, too, strains with his task.
Finally, my jaw gives way, and in a brief moment—faster than one of my shallow
breaths—I feel the wafer slide in. My mouth is held shut, and the tainted host
dissolves in the wetness of my saliva, held forever within me.

This was the most difficult memory to grasp. Speaking about it was unthinkable. Although
there was a ritual tone in several of the sexual abuse memories, this one was the most
gruesome, its content revoltingly unbelievable. Throughout the years, I have sought other
explanations for what is one of my clearest memories. It has been suggested that these
things are often staged to add leverage to threats for silence, keeping the victims in line.
I cannot say for sure what is true. All I know is what I remember through the eyes of a
young traumatized child . . . . and the memory of that has haunted all the days of my life.

Food has been used as a spiritual binding agent throughout the ages, being given in a ritual
"feeding" within a religious ceremony. Was forcing this host into me the ultimate attempt
to gain power over me? As with Persephone, was it intended to seal my connection to the
Underworld? Such an overpowering stance certainly kept the priests in a place of ultimate
power—able to seemingly take away life in a mere moment.

Sanctuary or Sacrifice?

I lived across the street from my church and school until I was eleven. My mother told me
that, during the time of the abuse, I would often be gone for hours without more than a
vague explanation of where I had been: "down the street" or "at the park." Having three
younger children in her care prevented my mom from being able to search for me, and of
course, she had no reason to believe that I was in danger. The small scope of our neighbor-
hood seemed relatively safe; the gravest concern was for cars coming down the street

during a curb-to-curb ball game or somebody slipping off a garage roof that served as our fort. No one thought about predators, and certainly no one questioned our safety when in the care of priests or nuns.

Having started school early, I was a year ahead of my classmates, and loving to read and write, I was a curious, intuitive six-year-old at the very top of my class. It was while I was being prepared for First Holy Communion in second grade that the first incident of sexual abuse on the altar occurred. Soon after that, the worst psychic abuse—the ritual with the tainted host—altered forever my connection with the Church. Guilt for not being able to prevent that horrible thing from happening followed me for most of my life. In a typical child-like response to abuse, I internalized the responsibility for what had been done to me. Powerlessness expressed in my scream dreams (I was unable to scream in order to summon help), and shame expressed in the bathtub scenarios (I thought I had killed someone and then forgotten about it). Abusers often leave deep and lasting emotions as a burden within the psyches of their victims.

In writing this book, once I recorded my own experiences without external influence, I spent over a year in research. One woman's experience touched me more than any other. Kathleen M. Dwyer remembers her father taking her to the side door of her church, bringing her to the lower level and into a room she had never been in before. Her memories, like mine, contain the secret basement ritual space. Dwyer's father brought her to the church when no formal activity was occurring, and a group of "fathers" placed her on the altar, removed the white slip they had dressed her in, made her kneel down and bend over, and then they raped her. In her own words, she says, "Increasing the terror and horrifying images of that night were the memories of my kitten, Snowball, being sacrificed in a perverted version of the Eucharistic sacrifice."

Dwyer calls her experience "ritual, sexual, and spiritual abuse done in the Catholic God's name, a perverted version of liturgical rite."[18] Dwyer specifically says this was not "satanic abuse (devil worship)," but I question how we can actually judge the nature of their intent.

Certainly, this secret ritual practice was outside mainstream Catholicism. I remember the eyes that glowed red while threatening to take my soul. Are those the frightened memories of a young, religious child, the manifestations of a twisted bishop, or "Satan" showing himself through psychic possession of a perverse priest? In a patriarchal hierarchy that strongly focuses a rigid dichotomy of good and evil, I wonder about the part that "evil" plays in it.

We know that horrific things have been done, repeatedly, by people convinced that their God approved of their actions. And in many cases, a bloody sacrifice is thought to organize and empower evil. As one who was the virgin blood sacrifice on the altar, I shudder to think about it, while I question whether the priests were conscious of their evil, or in some demented way thought they were still doing "God's work." I wonder if a child taken forcefully by the flesh of the priest or priests on the sacred altar is considered an offering to God in the hopes of forgiveness and redemption.

The Feminine Influence

Within the #2 Key to Wholeness, we recognize the feminine influence, both within ourselves and within our world. Many of us believe that the feminine influence is rising and becoming much more apparent. We are not meant to live exclusively under either masculine or feminine energies, but rather to cultivate a fluid balance of the two, allowing the Sacred Marriage of the Masculine and the Feminine to express through us, birthing and rebirthing, individually and collectively.

Historical reports of the establishment of patriarchal dominance note its occurance as taking place over 4,000 years ago. Yet, in spite of being repressed, feminine imaginal energies still exist, and Her nuances continue to collectively impact us. In an intriguing sequence of events reported by journalist Kate Osborn in the midst of the first major pedophile priest scandal, the incongruence of Cardinal Bernard Law, former archbishop at the basilica of *Our Lady of Perpetual Help* church in Boston, was exposed when many lawsuits accused him of failing to protect the children in his care. Law was the only U.S. bishop to resign over mishandling sexual abuse, publicly admitting to aiding and abetting 80 pedophile priests by transferring them from one parish to another.[19] His own Bostonian priests and the laity forced him to resign in disgrace, but Pope John Paul II elevated him as the Archpriest of the "mother of all basilicas." Law was appointed the head of *St. Mary Major* basilica in Rome. I find it interesting to note that both the Boston church, *Our Lady of Perpetual Help*, and the basilica, *St. Mary Major*, refer to the Divine Mother.

In his fascinating book, *The Alphabet Versus the Goddess*, Dr. Leonard Shlain points out that the human brain was reconfigured during the rise of alphabetic literacy, bringing about profound changes in history, religion, and gender relations. Dr. Shlain tells us that preliterate cultures were principally informed by holistic, right-brain modes that venerated the Goddess, maternal images, and feminine values. He notes that writing pushed cultures toward linear left-brain thinking and this shift upset the balance between men and women, initiating the decline of the feminine and ushering in patriarchal rule. Shlain examined the cultures of the Israelites, Greeks, Christians, and Muslims, contrasting the feminine, right-brained oral teachings of Socrates, Buddha, and Jesus with the masculine creeds that evolved when their spoken words were committed to writing. He points out that during the age of reasoning, the Divine Mother's image appeared everywhere in churches, communities, and homes, but although she was seen, she was not heard.[20]

We also know that Mother Mary has "spoken" through visions like the appearances at Lourdes. Has the feminine been pushed into the darkness of the unconscious and forced to communicate through subtle and often overlooked methods? Is she lost within the drone of raised, forceful voices from a demanding and rigid masculine Church hierarchy and its outer society? Could the feminine be the unseen psychic force that helped to finally expose the abuse of innocent children? Mother Mary is well known for her love of children, and the impact of public awareness concerning Cardinal Law's misconduct created a gaping fissure in the seemingly impenetrable protective armor of the Catholic Church. The facts were finally, and rather undeniably, laid out for public scrutiny.[21]

A distinct and powerful element of the overall patriarchy has been the disrespect of feminine influence. Unfortunately, as mankind has separated himself from the feminine, he has also denied a significant element of his own nature. One can reject and hide the truth, but one cannot destroy its existence; the expression of the feminine did not cease to be, but was simply hidden behind an elusive and sometimes very literal veil. Mother may have been silent, but She has remained powerfully present. And the time for her return is certainly at hand.

Returning to the Mother

In June of 2006, I attended a workshop facilitated by internationally-known Divine Feminine facilitators, Carolyn Muir[22] and Dr. Joan Heartfield[23]. Serving as the organizer and promoter for these workshops, I usually acted more as a support person to others with their process, rather than as a fully immersed participant. This time was quite different.

Having found kinship within this particular group of women, I spontaneously offered a song singing the names of the Goddess, as the freedom of the sweet melody flowed through me without reserve or shyness.

> *The violent wounding I sustained as a child has long ago been analyzed and filed in the bottom drawer of my internal realm. I rarely share any of the horrific details of my trauma. I feel the reality of it is a burden that others are not capable of bearing. I give my inner child the space to grieve from time to time. I feel as if I have given both the wounding and the healing all the attention they need. I am not ashamed. I don't question, "why me?" but instead have an odd kind of*

acceptance, sensing a deeper purpose. My past is the one that I have been given, and the memory of it is mine to carry. I understand and accept this.

In this women's gathering, the process we share is very sweet and caring. Within our sacred space, it is safe to simply "be." No need to feel pleasure or pain. Just give and receive, each one creating an unconditionally loving container for others, and also being held within a loving and supportive container. I have seen the transformative power this open space provides.

Tears surprisingly choke my throat as I strain to declare that I am ready for the enormity of joy, of love. I deserve it. It is mine. I really think I believe that, but something still guards the space normally reserved for joy. I can intellectualize but not embody this elusive sense of joy. And love, well . . . true love seems to be just beyond my reach.

I lie down to receive, unafraid. I know it's time, and I feel ready. At the last moment, I playfully dash off to get my licorice, my child-self peeking through. Nestling back within this sacred womb of love and acceptance, formed by sweet women, creates safety. The threads of our gifts are interwoven into a beautiful tapestry of interconnected purpose, which lies beneath me as a birthing blanket. I relax into the process, and at first, a very gentle and easy physical release moves through me.

Suddenly, torrents of physical sensations take over my body, bringing contortions that seem to originate from deep within my belly. I hear a blood-curdling scream from somewhere in the room and am momentarily pulled away with concern for whoever is screaming . . . .

I return with my awareness to my own body and follow the energetic trail I feel within me. I track it coming from deep within my belly, moving up through my heart, up through my throat, and finally sliding right out my mouth. Oh, my, that brutal screaming is coming from me!

I would never scream. I can't scream . . . I've tried.

Again and again. Again and again. Then, a towel placed in my hand. Use this. Permission to scream. Now I do it consciously, by choice. It feels like five minutes pass as I let outrageous screams, stifled for so long, finally find their path of escape. I remember long ago feeling as if I was being killed; the sheer terror of the memory returns to me. I remember, but I am not consumed by my fear because through little slits of squinted eyes I can still see the beautiful women's faces watching me, caring for me, supporting me. They look at me with concern and love. "I am fine," I say, and I know that I am.

But there's more. A gentle stroking on my throat to ease the paths of my screams unexpectedly coaxes out a powerful image of a grey serpent. He seems dark and ominous. I feel him forcefully slither from my body, moving out of my mouth . . . could this be the remnant of a child's memory of a penis shoved down her small throat?

My mother gave me her body for nine months to incubate and birth me into this world. But that day, my body and soul were called to a re-birthing. I had six sacred attendants who helped me push through my labor, and the next day the menstrual blood came—a divine feminine flow, cleansing and blessing the path once wounded and now free. Blood, red and pure, alive and well; vibrantly healthy. This natural process encouraged me, connecting me from one woman to the next and the next, within a vast and boundary-less sisterhood. Overflowing with a sense of belonging, I wrote the following poem:

Listen to the Call

There is a primordial scream
            rising from deep within woman bellies . . . .
                        Can you hear it?
It reverberates through the land in many forms
            seen and unseen,
                        heard and unspoken . . . .
It is the deep ache of the loss of a mother—known, but forgotten.

She is calling us—the Divine Mother.
She calls us from within ourselves,
            beckoning us back to our true nature,
                        the order of the Divine Woman.
There is no one religion, or practice, that we need to embrace . . . .
                        The path is a way of being.

Listen to the call.
Bring it forth, in your own precious way.
Honor that which is "woman" . . .
            and see the great change that it brings to the world.[24]

Gentle, Loving Presence

As is life's perfection, I was drawn to help promote Carolyn and Joan's work, leading me toward a powerful and pivotal healing. I will be eternally grateful. I also was attracted to many, many years of energy studies, which led to my being a teacher of conscious energy studies beginning in 1990.

Years ago, while facilitating an attunement (or energetic initiation) in the ancient tradition of Reiki, I experienced an extraordinary visitation. The purpose of the attunement is to open the receiver to more directly channel Universal Life Force Energy for clearing, relaxation, increased vitality, and healing on many levels.

On more than one occasion, as I perform this profound attunement process,
I notice a figure in the corner of the room. I recognized him immediately as Jesus,
the Christ.

Since I have not thought too much about Him since my days with the Catholic
Church long ago, I know he can't possibly be there for me, so I assume that He
must be there for my student. Although our eyes meet, we never speak, and as I
walk to the front of the initiate, I literally and symbolically turn my back on Him.

When I see him appear again today, I distinctly observe his gaze, truly meeting
Him for the first time. And His gentle and curious look is seemingly quite patient
with me. I defiantly ask, silently, within my own mind,

"What DO you WANT?"

Without hesitation, in the most indescribably accepting and loving voice, He says,

"We are so proud of you!"

Those amazingly gentle, piercing eyes penetrate right into me, with waves of
indescribable, unconditional Love. Uncharacteristic tears make their way down
my cheeks as He quickly declares,

"They had no right to use my name."

I had no clear memory of it, but this mystical experience with Jesus told me that they had
used His name in perpetuating the abuse; it was mistakenly Jesus, and the Church, that I
held accountable. Even though the church leadership as a whole does have some responsibility for how they handle what happens within their walls, it is important to recognize
that each individual within the church is responsible for his or her own behavior with
regard to child abuse. The abuser and his supporters are the ones responsible.

And we are each responsible for how we treat our own wounds. By accessing the profound energies available through Key #2, you can open to the potential of a new birth. And in Key #3, we will explore what you can do to bring further healing into your own life.

The Sacral Chakra for Healing

> Your living is determined not so much by what life brings you
> as by the attitude you bring to life;
> not so much by what happens to you
> as by the way your mind looks at what happens.
>
> ~ Kahlil Gibran

In one form or another we, like Persephone, each traverse the perilous path from ignorant (sometimes blissful) innocence to a mature and more consciously aware reality. As we personally acknowledge and experience both the light and the dark, we discover an evolved, richly integrated way of being. In our Western culture, we may be less conscious of this melding, but it remains a factor in our personal and collective evolution. We are challenged to meet our own light and dark, both conscious and unconscious, in order to heal ourselves at the root and core.

You may have been abused in a manner similr to what I experienced, or your wounds may be of a completely different nature. Perhaps you have not suffered child abuse, but rather have been tossed about by life's challenges and turmoil. Whatever is your reality, it matters. Pain matters regardless of its form, and if it is lasting pain, then it deserves to be listened to, dealt with, and comforted. By having the courage to face your own darkness, embracing your own wounds and clearing the limiting threads that still bind you, you contribute healing to the whole.

Know that what you do affects every other one of us, abused or not. I appreciate your brave efforts and support your personal process. And even without knowing the details of your story, I truly can say that I understand at least some of what you are going through. Keep moving, and you will find a guiding light leading to transformation. This light may appear in the form of those who offer assistance to help heal the remnants of what harmed you, and it may also be the deep sense of knowing that wells up from within you, helping you to sort out what is the truth and what are the illusions that you were force-fed.

Shame

> Perhaps all the dragons in our lives are princesses
> who are waiting to see us act, just once, with beauty and courage.
> Perhaps everything that frightens us is, in its deepest essence,
> something helpless that wants our love.
> ~ Rainer Maria Rilke[25]

One of the most common emotions trailing behind any form of abuse is a sense of shame. The abused often blames themselves, rather than confronting the idea that a parent or caregiver, loved one, or even a stranger could *do* such a thing without provocation or cause. "Certainly there must be something I did to make this happen," is a common thought. Society as a whole often attacks victims rather than face taking the necessary steps to try to stop perpetrators. And when the victim is a young child and the perpetrator a respected adult, the issue is even more charged.

Healing shame happens within you. Although those who support you can add to the potential for healing shame, you must make the choice to explore those thoughts and feelings that keep shame in place. Shame is not necessarily sharp and debilitating; yet, it is devastating no less. At times, it may be a chronic dull ache, a deep sense of not being good enough, or a belief that you are tainted or spoiled in some way. For me, shame was that feeling that something about me was not quite right, not quite whole.

- Do you feel ashamed about something that happened to you?
- Do you feel a strong sense of shame without knowing why?

Dis-membering and re-membering your self:

- Is there an experience that you pretend did not happen?
- Is there a personal trait that you pretend does not exist?
- Is there a part of you that is walled off and banished from the rest of your core self?
- Are there parts that need to be welcomed and integrated into the whole of you?

Re-gaining trust:

- Are you able to embrace the trust and abandon of the innocent child within you? Or are you braced for what life brings you each day?
- What would it be like for you to trust more fully? What would it be like to really let go and allow the natural flow of life? Can you even imagine it?

Connecting with guidance:

- Are you aware of your inner guidance?
- Do you trust in your inner guidance?

Try to open to each experience as an opportunity for growth and expansion. I want to be perfectly clear—in no way am I condoning abuse or excusing abusers from their responsibility for what they have done. I am simply saying that once we have lived through the terror and the horror of the experience, it is, at least partially, our choice how we then handle the aftermath. One of the most powerful stances a victim can take is to stand up to the abuser (who lives on within her) and say clearly and with conviction,

"You no longer have dominion over my life. I, myself, *choose* how to live!"

It is also powerful for you to choose to actively mine gems of insight that lie undiscovered within you. Find some useful aspect in all of the hurt and craziness, thereby softening whatever has been the lasting blow and instead processing your pain into strength. Do not downplay the occurrence of your trauma, but instead begin to rework the old images, looking to the potential value of their meaning in the overall scheme of your life. Rather than adopting a negative trajectory based on abuse, create pathways for successful living filled with hope and trust in the potential of what is to come. Use your creativity to re-frame the idea of wounding as something absolutely terrible that happened *to* you, which left you powerless to deal with its harshness and hurt. Remember that any betrayal, abuse, trauma, or suffering is only one part and not the totality of who you are—the truth of your essential core self is *so much more* than that limited scope. The dragons and demons within you are awaiting you to slay them, so they can be reborn as something beautiful and brave!

Seeking Understanding

We find a deep understanding by exploring the parts of ourselves: both light and dark, obvious and hidden, conscious and unconscious. After my tainted communion experience, I was in this world, but not of it. Even though I was considered a stable person, gratefully not captive in the chronic despair or the serious mental illness that befalls many abuse victims, I still awkwardly navigated a landscape of shifting inner realities. At times, I dealt with what was before me—rightfully present to my daily life. At other times, I dealt with the unseen demons that haunted me in the form of inappropriate suspicion, distrust (never believing I could *really* trust anyone), insecurities, and the perpetual belief that no one would ever love me. During these shaky times, nothing in physical reality could convince me otherwise or ease the sense of betrayal superimposed as an imprint onto my outer reality of life.

On the other hand, I also learned as a child that there were unseen forces and spiritual guides there to protect me. Being able to hear, see, and depend on that other dimension from a young age led me to wholeheartedly trust in knowing that the open portal to God was not found in an external, sacred place or through the teachings of an elevated master teacher, but instead was, forever, in me. This spiritual freedom directed my life and my life's work. Depth psychologist Carl Jung infers that the descent into chaos is perilous but can yield great rewards when he says, "If one opens up chaos, magic also arises."[26] For me, the invaluable gift was the strong and easily accessible relationship I developed with the spiritual guides through a deep connection with my own inner realm.

2nd Key to Wholeness: returning to the mother and birthing ourselves

Within the Sacral Chakra live the polar opposites of the feminine and masculine energies. It is also within this #2 chakra that we can return to the Divine Mother and re-birth ourselves. Bring union into your life by exploring the powerful interaction of the feminine meeting the masculine and the masculine meeting the feminine. By acknowledging and utilizing both influences, we birth anew through a united connection with the fullness of our human potential.

Try using this affirmation to welcome your day:

> I start this day anew. Today is an opportunity for things to change in my life.
>
> I reach inside of me to find the nurturing mother, and I draw her close. She offers me the greatest protection—from the inside out. She is supportive of all I do, fierce in her commitment to me.
>
> I reach inside of me to find the nurturing father, and I draw him close. He offers me the greatest protection—from the inside out. He is supportive of all I do, fierce in his commitment to me.
>
> A lack of love may have kept me small; fear and insecurity limited my belief in who I am and what I am. I open this day to all that life has for me. With the love and support of the nurturing mother and the nurturing father, I am strong in who I am and what I am. I am strong in all that I have to do.
>
> I open to receive the communion of my own soul as I embrace my day with great expectation and joy for life itself. The great web of life supports me in all of my endeavors as I stretch into all that I can be. I am confident and assured as I relax into the flow of life. It is good to be alive!

Include the following meditative focus whenever you would like to acknowledge or activate the second chakra and the #2 Key to Wholeness:

Imagine a strong cord of brilliant red light moving from the base of your spine, the coccyx, down through both legs, and into the earth. Breathe slowly, in and out, for three or four breath cycles.

Now, see the vibrant orange hue of the Sacral Chakra moving through your lower belly and downward as it partners with the red cord, moving together, separate yet harmonious, moving downward, and connecting you with the ground beneath you. Speak the following statement with a strong, yet gentle voice to invite activation and to embrace the support of this significant healing center:

The Sacral Chakra connects me with my sensual nature. I find pleasure in what I see, touch, smell, taste, and feel. And I recognize my sexuality as another sensual opportunity for Spirit expressing in form through my physical body. Whether I chose to share my sexuality with another or remain celibate, I recognize it as a human gift.

I acknowledge and open to healing any sense of shame. I open to receive my fullest good every day as I draw on the support of the Divine Masculine and the Divine Feminine in balance and harmony. I stand with a strong pelvic base and engage the second chakra to help me channel and ground inspired creativity in all areas of my life. I reach beyond any limits I now experience into the vast expanse of my truest potential.

3rd Key

Discovering Meaning
and Life Purpose

You've seen my descent, now watch my rising!

~ Rumi

Life brings the experiences we need
in order to set us up for the healing that we will discover.

~ Donna DeNomme

The *Manipura* Chakra supports me with a powerful force radiating from my own center in the middle of my solar plexus to all the other parts of me, inside and out. This vital life force beckons me to fulfill my life purpose, and feeds me daily with the inspiration and strength to accomplish what I have come here to do. I digest all that happens to me physically, mentally, and spiritually with an appropriate balance, finding the meaning and purpose in both my challenges and my successes. I stay strong because I am fed from the inside out and driven by a trusted, creative force that directs me toward success no matter what challenges come my way. Life is an unfolding adventure of my core Soul Self evolving through human form.

The 3rd Key to Wholeness unlocks the realization that all of life has purpose and that we are tempered into our individual shape and form through life's ordinary and extraordinary experiences. Everyday occurrences and once-in-a-lifetime happenings all have significance! How we respond to what we have been given is vitally important, too, as we can unlock greater understanding about who we are by examining what we do with life's challenges and successes. We can build our character by choosing to take on a new lens, or by cleaning the old one through which we have been seeing the world.

The 3rd Key to Wholeness, located in the solar plexus, celebrates the understanding that instead of there being one "right" way to heal, there are many paths of healing and many methods that can help you develop and express your unique wholeness. Life is about discovering and having the courage to claim *your* path. The solar plexus chakra is the perfect center for recognizing your own personal power and will to thrive—the desire and the intention to become the very best that you can be! By drawing in practitioners who practice modalities that support self-reflection and healing, you can ease the evolution of your awareness. Let's explore principles and modalities for enhancing the healing process. We also will examine the concept of the Wounded Healer archetype for bringing forth not only personal healing, but also collective change.

Keep Moving!

Why does one person heal and another cannot? What causes one to crumble when she encounters adversity and another to rise to the challenge? When we are wounded, the suffering of that wound, the drawbacks or limitations of its aftermath, and the tragedy of its occurrence are often apparent. What takes further examination is identifying what, if any, *value* there is in the wounding.

Where there is a wound, there is a way in to your deeper, inner self. Wounds pierce our outer, resistive shell into the very core of us—it is one reason they hurt so much. I believe that we all have the capacity to heal. Yet, unfortunately, many of us treat our wounds as issues to be avoided, in an attempt not to touch tender spots that still hurt. If we can realize that within a wound we often find the essence of our own personal magnificence, understanding our wounds becomes something to actively pursue. By really looking at our wounds, we can truly see them, comfort them, and nurture them through their process of transformation.

Recognize that this journey is a work-in-progress. At times you may find yourself in a heightened, very active, and highly transformative state, and change may occur very, very quickly. At other times, you may experience a slow and difficult crawl through a murkiness, dense with thick black goo. Yet, even in the slowest crawl, transformation is still at work below the surface. You have already survived. If your intention is to now rise above your wounding and soar into a successful and joyous life, just *keep moving* through the nasty stuff that appears to keep you stuck. Eventually the muck will clear, and, like the rainbow peeking through after a horrible storm, there will be a bright dawning over the next horizon.

"The Quickest Way Out Is Through . . . ."
~ My spiritual guides said (which is what kept me moving!)

Trust is an essential piece, one we learn again and again. As we navigate one layer, another presents itself. Developing the drive and direction to keep going may feel like stepping off a cliff into a dark abyss or moving into the woods without a lantern. Often it feels like we must continue without being able to see the path ahead. Navigate your twists and turns knowing that if you are pointed in the right direction, all you have to do is keep moving and trusting in the perfection of your process. Sometimes it may feel like two steps forward and three back, but as long as you are moving toward healing, there is growth, so for goodness' sake, don't stop! Keep on going; each effort matters, and every step counts.

So many of the words the spiritual guides said to me during my healing continue to ring true, influencing the very essence of who I am and the core of all I do. One such essential statement is,

"The Point Is Not The Wounding; The Point Is In The Healing."

This hopeful encouragement came constantly over a period of years. Over and over it repeated, becoming a mantra within me—urging me to look for more, to search for and embrace the bigger picture with greater meaning. It is the truth for all of us: we are evolving toward wholeness. Inner guidance seeks to lead us to higher and higher levels of expression in an ever-evolving, upward spiral.

My early adult years were pivotal healing times, bringing forth my own personal healing as well as directing me onto the path of the healer through which I would assist others. I recognize that all healing is self-healing and that my role is simply to help others to find their own innate ability to heal. Often, all one needs is a marker pointing the way and perhaps encouragement for taking those initial steps.

So walk with me for just a little bit, on the winding path I followed toward healing. Perhaps you may catch a reflection of your own healing, or perhaps you may just know that I found my way into the darkness and *through* it. This understanding may in some way bring hope and encouragement.

I acknowledge the difficult landscape you must traverse. I can only imagine your wounding and your pain . . . but I know, absolutely, that within your journey of healing there is meaning and great value. There is a point to your wounding—and that point is found in the healing. So step with me onto the Path of the Healer, and begin by reaching in for what hurts and cradling that which needs healing within you.

Insight Out

Every situation, properly perceived, becomes an opportunity. . . .

- Helen Schuman[27]

The Healer does not judge what a situation or a physical imbalance looks like in an attempt to "fix it" or alleviate the resulting pain or turmoil. We can only show up with a willingness to meet the difficulty and allow healing to unfold. We open to recognize vital clues pointing us toward the insight held within the trauma. And often we may not know the final outcome when we begin, but instead we surrender and trust in the journey as it happens. Life transforms when the path of healing is embraced. If you cannot hold the possibility of this truth for yourself, or if the pain and fear surrounding your trauma is still overwhelming, seek out a professional to support you. A worthwhile counselor or coach can be a valuable guide, allowing you to chart your own course, but helping you to navigate the trail.

I believe we all are "healers" in our own way. Whether your life holds a desire for service to others in the form of being a professional practitioner or not, you can still hold an intention to be a healing influence. How do you react when someone around you is facing a life challenge or an emotional pain? Are you able to stand with them in the face of their difficulty? When our own pain is still unmet and our inner challenges unresolved, sometimes we are unable to be there for others in their times of need. Perhaps the time is ripe for you to do some deep inner work. I encourage you to draw in your support, professional and personal, so that you can move through the trauma that still lives within you and discover the vast potential that lies just ahead on the other side.

Body Wisdom

The body possesses a natural wisdom. If we stay present to what and how the body feels, observing physical symptoms, we can read these valuable guideposts to discover what is out of balance mentally and emotionally, too.

Kinesthetic communication is also a factor, because we may "feel" pain or discomfort in our bodies when we have something deeper out of balance. And the body shares what the mind is not yet ready to think about or verbalize. Bodies hold the burden of wounding in the form of physical imbalance or dis-ease, and through our focus on these outer symptoms, we can learn more about and navigate the inner realms.

If you are unfamiliar with this essential concept of the body mirroring the person as a whole, I suggest that you read Louise Hay's books, beginning with *You Can Heal Your Life*.

Catherine Ponder's *Healing Secrets of the Ages* can be very helpful, too. In keeping with our focus on utilizing the chakras for healing, I also recommend Deborah King's *Truth Heals,* as it is an excellent and engaging reference for identifying which chakra is out of alignment and striving to create balance. Affirmative prayer and spiritual coaching can be a good addition to any wellness plan, as they help facilitate a shift in your "mental equivalents," or what you believe is true. When inner beliefs shift, so does our outer reality.

We must pay attention to the body and give it what it needs, or like a child it will act out, demanding our attention. Just this week, I met with a colleague who was on crutches. When I questioned her about it, she said that she had been getting some deep bodywork to address problems on her right side. She began to feel her left side nudging her for attention, and after ignoring the nudge for several weeks, she fell down a few stairs and tore her left meniscus. Now certainly she is attending to the right *and* the left!

When we cultivation attention and intention to heal the outer, the inner shifts as well. Healing modalities that focus on root causes rather than treating surface symptoms are the most effective form of treatment. There are many trained professionals (in a variety of bodywork practices) who can be invaluable anytime, but especially during heightened times of healing. I recommend that my clients receive bodywork treatments while they are addressing significant mental and emotional issues. Reiki, Healing Touch, Jin Shin Jyutsu, Shiatsu, or any form of massage can be nurturing and open the body to release what is held there. There are several forms of trauma-release therapy that are excellent, too. I found Network Chiropractic, as well as other chiropractic modalities and acupuncture (especially 5-Element Acupuncture), to be invaluable in not only easing my process, but also often facilitating it. Many deeper thresholds were crossed during "breakthroughs" experienced while engaged in various treatment modalities.

Our physical body, with the body wisdom it possesses, connects to our unique and precious individual ego. In our quest for enlightenment, we may wish to disconnect from the "separate" ego in order to connect with the higher vibrations of "oneness." We are in a time where we are challenged to live from the realization of our connection with all things, thereby ceasing, as a collective, from acting out in aggression toward another person, place, or thing. People can live with acceptance and compassion when they recognize the outside world as an extension of their inside world (see more about this in Key #7). In this worthy quest, the little ego is often shoved aside, left in the dust, or worse, targeted for annihilation. The ego is not bad—it simply has been overused and misused by us humans.

One priceless lesson I was taught by my Native American teachers is the art of neutrality. Neutrality is the ability to observe what is going on around us and still remain mentally, emotionally, and *energetically* clear—unattached from an ego place. We are not trying to impact or change what we are observing. We are not invested, instead allowing the subject of our attention to evolve naturally without our input. New Thought teachers often call this "the art of detachment."

On the other hand, our individual ego does play a useful part in our success, as it offers an important basic need—the drive to survive. Our physical body and body wisdom markers provide direction for our healing and also our thriving, too. A strong ego enables people to move through the very worst of trauma and to keep moving through the aftermath to the other side. It is only when we become stuck in this place of ego and mistakenly view the world from an "us over them" perspective that the ego becomes problematic. Many spiritual teachers have encouraged us to find balance with our egos because the Western world is ego-skewed, a common quality of our patriarchal structures.

As feminine energies re-emerge and we individually and collectively embrace each other, demonstrating the feminine qualities of inclusivity and diversity rather than hierarchal dominance, we may come into balance with our Collective Ego. Individually we can each contribute to this hopeful cause by meeting and dealing with our own ego struggles. Confronted by change, the ego feels as if it is dying and may lash out initially until it learns another way. Be patient with the ego as you move through this process.

As I was writing about my abuse, I felt my ego rise with overwhelming terror. The status quo of years of silence was being threatened. Old walls were coming down, and people could see into the dark and rotting flesh of long ago . . . some days, it was almost too much to bear—the resistance and the overwhelming fear of it. At times it felt like I would literally die in the process of this writing. So I contacted those I trust and shared what was happening. Times like these are not ones to maintain an outer stoic mask or to insincerely appear strong to those around you. It is also not the time to "throw yourself to the wolves" by sharing your inner turmoil haphazardly with anyone who will listen. Choose the very best people who possess the skills to help you through your rough patches. Select those who you know will stand by you. Don't let your ego swallow you, but rather help it to grow beyond its limited scope and view.

When I visited my deepest fear (that of speaking an unspeakable secret), I met my own terror. As I listened to those I drew in for support, the unbearable weight softened, and the inescapable sense of perishing eased. I still had to walk through the transformative fire, but these invaluable friends and colleagues covered me with a proverbial protective coat to keep me from being badly burned. Their continued consciousness focused on knowing the truth of my ability to pull this project together and lifted me up to complete the difficult task at hand. The drive came from deep within me; yet, it was enlivened through human interaction and support. Utilizing the "home team advantage," we can draw in those who will say, "Yes, keep on going. You are not going to die; you are only breaking through to the next level." Asking for help goes beyond the ego fear or ego perspective to embrace a greater sense of interconnection within community. When we embrace the ego and give thanks for its enduring strength, we can use its gifts from a place of balance, drawing on its innate capacity without allowing it to run the show.

When we move beyond the ego, we connect with a greater reality than what is limited by our own little reality. We can open wider . . . feel more . . . and give more.

Healing Self / Healing the Collective

There is a paradox to our Universe. This paradox sets the stage for the necessity of our own individual healing, because it is our most potent opportunity to positively affect the whole. By meeting and dealing with our own wounds, we help to heal the wounds of our planet.

By meeting the dysfunctions within ourselves and our own families, we address the dysfunctions on our planet and help to tip the energetic scale, providing the space for collective healing.

No matter where you go, there you are. You cannot escape yourself. In the same way, you cannot escape your wounds or the need to heal them. Mystics and philosophers as far back as Plato and Pythagoras acknowledged the power of one who has been wounded turning her attention to healing. Victor Frankl, a psychiatrist who survived the Nazi concentration camps, inspired us with first-hand wisdom about drawing value from one's trauma. Frankl believed that suffering is a fundamental human experience, one through which we can discover great understanding about life's meaning.[28] Gandhi said, "Our greatness lies not so much in being able to remake the world as in being able to remake ourselves." And Thomas Holdcroft said, "Life is a grindstone. Whether it grinds us down or polishes us up depends on us." If there are untouched remnants from your past or present, if there are places you would like to improve to be more in alignment with your ultimate truth, turn your attention and your intention there. Make a difference for yourself. And make a difference for us all. Life is an ever-expanding adventure, leading us toward our necessary growth by opening unforeseen portals that contribute to our character development. At times, one relatively small act can bring forward great change.

Spirit Name brings Transformation

A major and pivotal shift for me involved receiving my spiritual name through a group I studied with for five years. This ceremonial-based community called Koda Maka (Earth Friend)[29] helped me to appreciate the sacred in every blade of grass, every tree or plant, every four-legged creature, every winged, every water being, and even the smallest creepy-crawly. I honor what provides me with nurturing substance, whether it is the food that I eat or the beauty I look upon. In appreciating every part of the natural world, one also gleans an appreciation of the masculine and the feminine, noticing how they complement each other in nature; without the other, each one would not survive.

After a time of mutual meditation and prayer in a sacred ceremony, the shaman gifted me the name that came to him in his vision—*Wakinyape Maka Wichinope*, Earth Star Rising. This name put me more directly in touch with my human manifestation in this world, while integrating it with the transpersonal, spiritual understanding I already held close. Up until this point, as I mentioned before, I had been in the world, but not really of it. This new spiritual name helped me to develop strong and resilient ties with the earth, claiming her as my mother, and also to understand that the quickest way out of this life was to successfully move through it, fulfilling my life purpose. As I developed a connection to all of life, there was newfound security in everything I did, which circled back and enhanced my personal happiness.

Embodying a Soul Truth

Through spiritual urgings and synchronistic events, I was naturally led to the right teachers, often living in simple ways in harmony with the earth and the natural world. They didn't have fancy offices or university degrees hanging framed upon their walls; yet, their teachings were more valuable to me than any found in great revered halls of learning. Their lessons introduced me to ancient lineages with ancestor energies to access. The scope of my support system increased with each passing year as I studied in Mayan, Peruvian, and Native American lineages. I did not take on teachers easily, because I learned at such an early age to listen within myself to the wise and helpful guidance channeled there. Now, that inner guidance led me to expanded study by providing powerful teachers in the outer world.

Often when I would connect with the right teacher or shamanic healer, she or he would already know that I was coming. Her guides had told her. Or his ceremony had indicated my arrival. To be recognized by a shaman is a powerful experience, one which is felt through every part of your body and soul, as there is a resonance of being in exactly the right space and time. Life shifts in powerful and profound ways.

If you desire such experiences, do not go out and search for them. Go into contemplation and prayer. Make offerings to Great Spirit as you commune with the earth and the natural world. Open yourself to possibility, and watch for the signs all around you indicating your most expansive direction . . . that which is yours will be drawn to you.

Shamans use their unusual ability for the "good of the people"—for the village or the community at large. The word *shaman* means "one who sees in the dark"[30] beyond the physical reality with a spiritual insight that often affords the ability to travel to spirit worlds, hidden from our usual view. Through their travels, shamans gain information and skills that help heal others by working in harmony with this spirit world. Being instructed in these ancient ways provided me with an extended sense of security, for the shamanic path was reminiscent of my earlier travels, my earlier instruction at the feet of my guides, and my flights on the wings of my spirit bird. Once again, I came to know that I was not alone on my path or in my experiences. I sometimes wonder why we, in our human evolution, seem to need to discover this truth over and over again—at least that is a lesson that I have had to learn, personally, again and again!

Shamanic "sight" may often involve seeing beyond the darkness of separation and isolation, the darkness of being misunderstood or misconstrued. By looking into that darkness, looking deep within its very eyes, and perhaps even seeing what it sees, we can learn to navigate through it. On the other side is union with the Divine. Knowing and trusting that there is much more beyond our physical reality can be pivotal to healing, especially when one has been ritually abused in a religious context (more about this in Key #6). For now, let me share the expansive understanding that came through my first *hemblecha*, a solo Vision Quest:

I'm instructed not to leave my circle, because it provides a strong energetic protection from wild animals and unseen spirits. As I watch my supporters descend down the mountain trail, I have already stepped through the spiritual threshold into an altered state of transition. Through weeks of preparation and prayer, I am open and ready.

The natural beauty surrounding me is awe inspiring. The Colorado Rockies are magnificent! I sit with anticipation for what will transpire. I knew at a young age the great potential held within ceremony and ritual, and I feel deeply connected with this particular ritual. I cradle my sacred ceremonial pipe within my arms, from time to time raising it upward and following its path with my gaze as I look to Great Spirit. I offer songs of gratitude and prayers for all of the people. I keenly observe my surroundings and myself. Sometimes the smallest movement or the quickest flash holds wisdom and understanding. The creepy-crawlies (ants and spiders) and mosquitoes come across the line of my sacred circle and then scurry right back out. It is clear from their movement that they feel this space has been sanctioned just for me.

The others down the hill are holding vigil, focusing on my safety and sending supportive energy. I am greatly empowered by their presence. Even though I am physically alone, I never feel isolated, but rather have an expanded sense of my connection with all-there-is, beginning with what is around me in the physical beauty of this place and moving way, way beyond to places on the planet where I have never been and will never go. I feel connected with all people and all things. I feel one breath, one heartbeat, One Spirit. I am exposed on the mountain, and yet I sit aligned with absolute trust. I have no fear.

In time, I begin to feel really, really sick. A well-meaning friend had told me to be sure to drink an electrolyte drink as my final meal before the Vision Quest, and the lemon-lime concoction did not sit well in my stomach. Its contents have long since passed through my system, as evidenced by the dry heaves I had when I first came on top of this mountain. Now, after a full day in the strong blaze of the direct sun, I feel extraordinarily weak. As I close my eyes, the world spins inside me, and I wonder if I might pass out or worse, perish. The air is completely still, and the sun is blasting hot. Sweat spills precious water from my empty system. I have been fasting for over 20 hours.

I hear a strange sound outside of me gently say, "I come to comfort you this day. . . ."

"I come to comfort you this day, for you have taught the little one, Weston, to call me by name, and long after you are gone, he will speak of me as friend."

A soft, cool breeze caresses my hair, moving slowly in and through with a comforting wisp of air. With gratitude, I understand that this gift is given because I have taught the little boy I nanny for to love instead of fear Brother Tate, the wind. When I first came to be with him, Weston would run away and hide whenever wind storms picked up in the foothills where he lives. Together we would sit for hours in his bedroom window seat, watching the playful escapades of the wind dancing through the pine trees and the sage brush. Now the wind supports me as a welcomed ally in my time of need. I am grateful and offer a song to the wind and all that surrounds me . . . .

Many things both seen and unseen support us within a sacred ritual. Sunrise is astounding as a brilliant display of gorgeous reds and yellows mixed in the palette of a cloudless sky of pale and rich blues. The arrival of the sun seems quite miraculous after a long dark night! I watch the little creatures awaken to their day, and even though they only come so close, I am pleased with their company. Without any walls to separate me from this natural expanse, I am literally open and receptive to what this day will bring. Not only do I feel as if I know every blade of grass and every tree that surrounds me, but as I greet the light of the new day, my eyes look outward to the sky and all that is beyond it. Any sense of separation from the entire universe has been shed with the salt of my sweat. I float in a receptive and numinous state of consciousness, aligned with All.

Immersed in this elevated state, I am startled with a vision of a lone woman dressed in a long white leather fringed robe. Ptesan Wi (White Buffalo Calf Woman) stands a short distance away in the trees. Her beauty and presence are indescribable. My inclination is to stand with respect, but I am afraid if I move she will disappear. Her dark hair frames intense eyes that look upon me with scrutiny, looking into my deepest and most personal places. She scans my character in a millisecond, and her gaze softens. Her eyes let me know I am fine, so I sit still, hardly breathing. After a moment, the Calf Woman is joined by the lady in blue, the Virgin Mary, and then, Kuan Yin.

Could this be the very tired projections of my own mind? Mary is familiar to me from my Catholic upbringing, but until this morning I have not known Kuan Yin. She is introduced to me by her sisters. The three wise ones smile upon me with such sweet acceptance. And then, they move toward one another . . . blending into one form.

To this day, I believe that these precious feminine deities are one unified Spiritual Energy with three distinct manifestations. All three of them are dear to my heart, shining examples of how we might serve with compassion, healthy boundaries, and love. Malidoma Somé describes ritual as, "above all else, the yardstick by which people measure their state of connection with the hidden ancestral realm . . . ."[31] With sincere gratitude, I give thanks for these Divine Feminine ancestors.

In ritual we must always be open to what shows up, with or without our invitation, seemingly wanting to participate. Whether the information is given in the form of the mosquito that flies into the circle, pauses, and then flies out, the sound of the voice and movement of the wind bringing comfort, or the divine feminine ancestors, each piece is meaningful and significant. Malidoma Somé reminds us to draw "from nature and the cosmos life-essence that seeks to align itself . . . ."[32] In *Rites and Symbols of Initiation*, Mircea Eliade speaks about initiation rites as a "revelation of one's true self . . . It includes the opening up of the inner life of the spirit and releasing the potentials and possibilities within the individual."[33]

Ritual is a way of becoming clear and then, from that clarity, speaking our intention. Yet, it is also so much more—we physically and emotionally *embody* our intention. Ritual allows us to both ask for help from others and to offer our assistance to the greater plan. It helps us view the world spiritually as something we are aligned with, not for personal gain, but rather for a larger purpose. We develop different constructs to gauge our success; we define success by what we do to contribute, rather than what we "get" from our contribution.

Ritual also takes us out of our microcosmic selves and into the bigger understanding of our interconnectedness with all things. This interconnection with all of life translates into an understanding of our human need for one another. Many of us take the stance that whatever life brings, we can tough it out. "I'm strong. I don't need any help. I'm self-sufficient. I can do it alone." Maureen Murdock calls this the "machisma [machismo] code:"[34] the voice of the stereotypical hero who is revered and deeply enmeshed in our culture. Within the ceremonial circle, individual boundaries (representing independence) are blurred, as we connect for the good of the whole (representing interdependence). Even when the ceremonial focus is on a particular individual as in the Vision Quest, it is seen within the context of the whole. Perhaps this interdependence is what Malidoma Somé finds missing when he identifies the "starvation of the soul" in the modern world[35]. Malidoma also notes that surely "there must be an indigenous person within each of us," longing for community connection and ritual celebration.

Regardless of gender, race, economic, or political differences, there is something magical that occurs when we gather for ritual. Precious personal transformations, as well as strong community contributions, are possible within the context of traditional and contemporary rituals. If you desire such learning and growth, begin by asking what you are looking for, and put out a universal call for the perfect teacher, guide, or mentor to help you with your unfolding purpose. These practices are not to be entered into lightly or for personal gain. They are to be respected and treated with reverence. To enter this realm "in a good way" brings us to a place beyond our personal boundaries (including those of our wounding) and into a greater potential. Limitations may be shed and our greater potential embraced. We literally turn inside out, so we might share the very best of what is on the inside of us with the outside world!

There are times when I am well aware of the ancestor's blood running through my veins, or when I can distinctly see and feel the presence of spirit helpers from the natural world. Ritual is as natural as breath, and like working with the patterns of our own breath, working with ritual can cultivate lasting healing and true transformation. Ceremony and ritual are ancient and contemporary, personal and communal, familiar and expansive; ritual brings us back into the very best part of our Essence, grounding it in the physical world.

The Role of the Wounded Healer

To hurry pain is to leave a classroom still in session.

To prolong pain is to remain seated in a vacated classroom

and miss the next lesson.

~ Yahia Lababidi[36]

Let me share my abrupt awakening into the realization of being a Wounded Healer.

We're sitting around a large wooden table discussing the project before us, and Bill Loving speaks from a position of authority,

"Donna, why I wanted you on this committee is because of the amazing depth and understanding you bring to ritual. I want that superb sacred quality that you bring designed into this curriculum."

Suddenly it hits me and shortly thereafter, I have to excuse myself to go to the restroom. In this miniscule cubby of a room, I pace back and forth, two steps at a time. Two small steps until I hit the outer boundary of the bare restroom wall; turn, pace two steps, as I nudge against the sink; turn, two steps to the wall again. Back and forth, back and forth . . . two pieces of understanding are migrating toward each other.

"So wait a minute," I think, "Am I drawn to ritual—because I was ritually abused?"

Is this why it's so powerful? When a person hires me to design a ritual, is it really all about me? Am I just pursuing something I need? Am I using it to heal me?

An overwhelming sense of guilt envelopes me in the silent din of that two-seater restroom.

Yes, of course I understood that there was some connection between my past and the person I had grown to be. When I was a student at Cornell University majoring in Human Development & Family Studies (with a focus on Adolescence), my course of study helped me to understand my own teenage rebellion and also helped me realize the previous wounding that led to my harsh acting-out behavior. When I worked with unwed teen mothers, I observed my own early pregnancy at just nineteen with an often unemployed, womanizing boyfriend who I eventually married and soon after, divorced. But up until this time, I did not fully comprehend or even question how my projected needs might have shaped my professional choices.

The *Wounded Healer* is a universal archetype psychologist Carl Jung referred to in its relevance to those in healing professions[37]. The idea originated in Classical Greek Philosophy with Chiron the Centaur, who was half man and half horse. Chiron shot an arrow, dipped in the poisonous blood of Hydra, which accidentally dropped downward and wounded him. As a god he could never die, but instead he suffered excruciating pain for the rest of his eternal days. Apollo and Artemis taught medicine to Chiron, and as he tried to find a cure for his own wound, he learned much about healing, ultimately becoming the wisest healer in Ancient Greece. And in teaching others about how they could heal, he found great solace. The Wounded Healer is empathetic because she knows first-hand about pain and suffering. Like Chiron, to experience the depths of our own pain may lead us to a greater understanding of and compassion for others. If we can become more aware of the meaning of our wounding and transcend the surface reality of it, we can migrate to the realm of greater purpose.

For years, I resisted the label of "victim," viewing it as a sign of weakness. As we move up the chakra column into the energy center of the heart, I will invite you, too, to explore this aspect of healing further. In this third chakra, the Solar Plexus chakra, let us recognize the value in accepting wounding as an integral piece of our development—one to be acknowledged for its inherent wisdom and hidden power. When we access the Wounded Healer within us, we can turn our attention to the work of healing ourselves and others. Isn't it clear that my childhood sexual and ritual abuse is a significant part of who I am? What unclaimed fragments have you left behind that are actually parts of your truest self? The lesson of Chiron teaches us that we can move into our pain, move through it, and transmute it into priceless knowledge.

The Wounded Healer is not just a psychological concept, but a respected shamanic one as well, as most shamans experience harsh personal challenges early in their lives—extreme trauma, abandonment, or life-threatening physical illnesses or injuries. Whatever the form, it is through these experiences that the shaman learns how to navigate through spiritual realms in order to help others.

Will your wounds serve a purpose? Or will the scars they leave simply be a form of disfigurement? Or worse still, do you perpetuate abuse or wounding by holding it within you and spinning in its destructive patterns, continually re-inflicting your initial wounds? When we seek the nuances of our destructive patterns, learn from them, and find ways to release what does not serve us, we bring about healthy change—we learn the art of spiritual transformation. This process is clearly an upward spiral that regenerates itself in greater and greater arcs when we engage with it; as we explore multi-dimensional levels, more and more wisdom opens to us. Our curiosity acts as a powerful intention, allowing us to shift the darkness into illumination.

Our intention helps shape form. Spirit is perfect and infinite, yet formless, until it manifests in the physical world through various means of expression. In both ancient shamanic practices and in contemporary times, one who works with healing modalities knows the power of intention to create form and uses it to assist in bringing forth healing.

Sometimes healing is like a new birth and other times, like a death. Birthing a new expression may mean dying to the old one in order to cleanse or make way for the new. In writing this manuscript, I literally purged old skin, initially on specific, key parts of my body, and eventually over most of my body. Exposing a fresh, outer layer was reminiscent of the transformation of a snake as she sheds her old skin in order to make room for the new one—a welcomed symbol of the transformation that I, too, was experiencing through the introspection required for writing about the 8 Keys to Wholeness.

I must be absolutely clear—the understanding of the Wounded Healer does not negate the wounding or in any way condone it. But you have already lived through the trauma and are on the other side of what happened to you; gratefully, you have survived. By being willing to put down the sad story of what happened to you and open to the potential of its greater purpose, you harvest the rich fruit that flourishes in its aftermath. The stinking substance of your traumatic experience has provided rich fertilizer for your inner soil, cultivating growth of the sweetest nature within you.

Please realize that this process takes time. Be patient with yourself as you move through your changes, and keep drawing in positive information and support. If we jump from the wound into positivity and pure acceptance, we may circumvent the true understanding of the meaning of our wounds. This process is not meant as a Pollyanna stance, making light of life's difficulties. We must first stay *present* with the wounding, exploring its details and nuances. This is why a trained professional as a guide can be invaluable. Counselors and coaches know there is a need to allow you to walk through your own process in your own time, rather than trying to rush your natural course and force the healing. Key #7 explores these concepts further when we look at how others can stand in the flame of transformation with us, bringing light and support through our dark night of the soul.

There is great value in the understanding of the Wounded Healer—and great responsibility as well. To stay stuck in your wounds is to miss the point, really. It gives power to the abuse (and the abusers) because what happened self-sustains, repeating familiar, hurtful patterns. Although individual scenarios may involve different people in different places, the themes are the same, and the situations are similar, keeping us stuck in a destructive groove. Do you see this destructive repetition in your life? Be honest in this moment of reflection, acknowledging each and every nuance of repetitive wounding and failure, and any lack of success that you wish you could change. Simply identifying stuck patterns begins to open them to the potential for shift and change. You have more power than you may know to create a happier, fulfilled life.

Manly Palmer Hall, in his classic book *Healing: The Divine Art* (1943) says,

> Plato taught by his example that man possesses within himself the power to cure the diseases of his body [and soul], that in the end, every man is his own priest, and every man is his own physician. Wisdom is a universal medicine, and the only remedy for ignorance, the great sickness of mankind. This is the doctrine of the mystics, the doctrine which they learned in the old temples; the doctrine which someday must be the foundation of all enlightened therapy.[38]

No one is meant to remain in his or her places of suffering, and in spite of all that has happened or is happening, life holds more goodness for you. And the efforts of your personal healing tip the balance for others, contributing to the collective good. My professional work utilized and benefited from what I learned through *all* of my experiences, including ritual wounding and ritual healing. I am grateful for my life. Many other journeys were possible. And in spite of any pain or torment, or perhaps because of it, this journey has held precious and priceless gifts. I know the same is true for you. You, too, have a destiny that includes health and well-being. This is the life you were born to live!

The Solar Plexus Chakra for Healing

The #3 Key for Wholeness is located at your solar plexus, midway between the navel and the sternum. This is a power center that fuels your metabolic fire, allowing you to feel vitally alive; it also is a gathering place where the pancreas processes, assimilates, and regulates blood sugar. With this key we can harness energy and convert it into action—conscious or unconscious. The third chakra can also assist you with the development of an appropriate personal will, learning to move from a desire to have power *over* someone to recognizing that true power stands in harmony with its surroundings. Personal power translates to a strong, resilient ability to deal with the enormity of what you have been given, finding a way to move through it and move on with the rest of your life.

The time is now. If you haven't already done so, listen to the fear and anger held captive in this center, and cut the codependent chords that bind you to your past or present wounds, digesting them by separating the useful nutrients of meaningful information and allowing the waste to move through and be expelled. This may be a process that takes some time, or if it has been in process for years, calling forth the power and the wisdom of the third chakra may enable you to truly move on. Before we venture up the rainbow chord to the center of the heart, if possible, dump what no longer serves you. Let your beauty shine through the yellow hue of this power center, bringing confidence and self-assurance. Know that your life truly matters, and we all need you to step into the fullness of your truest self. Put down the heaviness of your wounded armor and step forward feeling the freedom that comes from being much lighter.

3rd Key to Wholeness: discover meaning and purpose in your wounds

I am not what happened to me; I am what I choose to become.

~ Carl Jung

When we encounter difficulty that has been kept hidden or unexpressed, a process of awakening occurs, leading us to even *deeper* unexpressed pieces of ourselves. Often what has been hidden can be a great blessing. I have witnessed clients who tap into artistic genius and others who access their ability to give and receive love. We don't just wall off our wounds; we wall off and deny our truest gifts as well, for fear that we don't deserve them.

Spend some time exploring what you know about yourself and being open to what you don't yet know! The best tools I've found are meditation and writing. Choose a time each day when you won't be disturbed. Spend 10-15 minutes just sitting and being quiet. You can sit with your eyes closed or keep them open. If you choose an open-eye meditation, look at something soothing, like the vast sky or the beauty of a sunrise. You can light a candle and gaze at its warm flame. You can sit in complete silence or listen to a relaxing CD of ocean waves or nature sounds; Tibetan bowls, bells, and other sounds can also create a fertile environment. For this meditation, avoid CDs with singing or chanting so you can use your own mind as a blank slate:

- Sit for 10-15 minutes in a quiet meditative pose.
- Then, write without stopping (a stream-of-consciousness writing) for another 10-15 minutes.
- Write in paragraph or list form.
- Begin with what you know about your likes and dislikes, values, and beliefs.

- Record what comes to mind without concern for grammar, or punctuation, or organization of your thoughts. It is perfectly fine to jump all over the place. This is an initial gathering process.
- Also be open to anything that surfaces from within you, wanting to find its voice, pushing for recognition. These pieces might be outside the boundaries of your focus or your specific questions. Give them the opportunity to be recorded.

- Reflect upon your lists and paragraphs to identify what is most important to you.
- Be open to any new information or surprises.
- Begin to integrate this information into the choices you make.
- Use what you learn about yourself to bring your life into alignment with your deepest desires and your innermost longings.
- And need I say it, a trained professional coach or counselor can be invaluable as support for this work.
- Repeat this process often to allow for new information to surface.

- You can engage in this same contemplative process every day for a week or a month, or once a month, or once a quarter.
- Make a personal assessment in some form a regular part of your yearly practice

Treasure Chest: uncovering your hidden potential

Imagine or envision a strong and sturdy chest with a golden latch on its front. The beauty of the trunk has aged, its leather sides enhanced by polishing over time. And even though this trunk has been tossed around, its stamina is unbreakable. The outer core cradles inner gifts and treasures of unimaginable beauty.

With the radiant key to wholeness found in this power center, unlock the lock and open the latch, allowing its captive contents a path of escape:

- Fear may pop out first, because sometimes it is our fear that tries to help us avoid something painful.
- Anger may peer out into the world, because anger sometimes keeps our core self safe by lashing out at those around us, so they don't poke at our wounds.
- Keep looking deeper . . . .

- Inside that trunk is a jewel. Or maybe two or three. Perhaps even more.
- Inside that trunk are disconnected and unclaimed parts of you—strengths and talents not yet manifested. They are the parts of you that are yet-to-be—riches beyond measure.
- Give them a little space to stretch and yawn. They have been captive for a very long time.
- Take them by the hand and venture out into the world. Allow them to explore and play, as you let yourself experiement with these new aspects to see what they can offer you.

- Allow this process of discovery space and time to unfold. Once you open the trunk, your inner gifts and talents can run free!
- Choose this time to get to know more of who you are, knowing the perfect time is now.
- Trust in the ultimate value of your life . . . there is so much more to you than even you know.

Personal Drive and Personal Renewal

I give myself the gift of freedom from the past, and move with joy into the now.
~ Louise Hay[39]

Personal drive is an interesting measure of the health and vitality of the third chakra energy. Do you balance your personal will and drive with an ability to relax and renew? As a wounded child, I was a highly driven, straight-A student who put myself through college as a single mother, winning a partial scholarship to Cornell University. At Cornell, I juggled a demanding academic load along with working full-time and helping to run the school for gifted children that my five-year-old attended. I also taught there. For years, if something was recorded in my day timer as an activity happening that day, I would attend, whether or not I wanted to go. I was driven to do it all in an effort to succeed. The need for outer approval and validation indicated an out-of-balance third chakra. Of course, the opposite can also emerge—it may be difficult for you to get out of bed in the morning. If your burden is overwhelming and life seems extraordinarily bleak, reach out to ask for help. There is so much more to life when we bring our powerful will center into a finely tuned balance of personal drive and personal renewal.

Epictetus (Epic-tee-tus), a Roman Stoic, professed that personal philosophy was not just a theoretical discipline, but a way of life. In essence, he was saying to "walk your talk" by being true to your own beliefs and desires! Epictetus conveyed our responsibility to contribute our own thoughts and actions to the aftermath of unchangeable life tragedies. In all of life's occurrences, those we accept and those we resist, it is necessary to add our authentic energies to the mix:

> Now is the time to get serious about living your ideals. Once you have determined the principles you wish to exemplify, abide by these rules as if they were laws, as if it were indeed sinful to compromise them.

> Don't mind if others don't share your convictions. How long can you afford to put off who you really want to be? Your noble self cannot wait any longer.

> Put your principles into practice—now. Stop the excuses and the procrastination. This is your life!

> You aren't a child anymore. The sooner you set yourself to your spiritual program, the happier you will be. The longer you wait, the more you will be vulnerable to mediocrity and feel filled with shame and regret, because you know you are capable of better.

> From this instant on, vow to stop disappointing yourself. Separate yourself from the mob. Decide to be extraordinary and do what you need to do—now.[40]

Imagine the red ray of the first power center grounding you into the earth beneath you. Imagine the orange ray of the second power center moving downward as it invigorates your creative ability to manifest a healthy life, and imagine the yellow ray rising within your solar plexus and joining the orange ray and the red ray, adding its unique fullness to the mix. Repeat the following affirmative blessing:

The Solar Plexus Chakra supports me with a powerful force radiating from the center of my core and stretching into all parts of me, bringing vital life force to awaken and enliven my true purpose. The energy of this center feeds me daily with inspiration, strength, and vibrancy to do what I have come here to do. I am fed from the inside out, digesting all that has happened to me, and all that is happening to me physically, mentally, and spiritually. No matter what challenges come my way, I am driven by a trusted, creative force that comes to me and through me, directing me toward success.

4th Key

The Survivor Embraces
the Victim

Your vision will become clear

only when you can look into your own heart.

Who looks outside, dreams.

Who looks inside, awakes.

~ Carl Jung

In the *Anahata* or Heart Chakra, I encounter comfort, forgiveness, and an opening to the greater potential beyond my wounds. I breathe easily and fully into the nurturing warmth of my own heart center, taking in vital life force energy for every part of my body and soul. I anticipate the good that comes my way, daily, as I relax into the Divine Flow, embracing and celebrating life. I marvel at life's transformative adventure as my life unfolds anew in remarkable ways. I am healthy, vibrant, and fully engaged in the wonder of my life.

The 4th Key to Wholeness is the strong and resilient Heart Chakra. The Heart Chakra may seem tender and sensitive, but it also contains a vast and powerful potential to heal, making it strong beyond measure. How we deal with what happens to us is a factor that helps define not only our character, but often our life's trajectory as well. Holding steadily to the awareness that the point is in the healing (not the wounding) allows us to accept all facets and all stages of our healing process. We can love each part of us, even those parts still in the process of awakening. It is through that portal of curiosity and acceptance that we discover our most integrated healing—and when one's heart does heal, it has an impressive capacity to regenerate, renewing faith in life itself.

A Dolphin Embrace

My guarded and constricted heart first began to open through a remarkable encounter with a female dolphin. For six years, I led trips to the beautiful island of Isla Mujeras, Mexico, creating many fond memories in the warmth of the Caribbean sun. None was as delightful as my very first encounter with the dolphins!

I offer a beloved song given to me by one of my dearest teachers. My morning meditation with my inner council was clear: sing your power song under the water! With my mouth open in order to attempt to do so, it sounds a lot like "blub, blub, blub" instead of the song's normal melodic chant. Still, it seems of interest to the water beings, because after one or two "blubs," I see a dolphin hovering in front of me, her entire body just inches away. She looks at me with fascination as she cocks her head from side to side. The dolphin's world is shaped by sound, and they are extremely sensitive to vibration, so I guess it makes sense that she is attracted to my strange underwater music.

Later in the day, we move to a naturally shallow pool, and I continue to commune with this same dolphin, stroking her soft skin and sharing energy with her. She snuggles in, moving closer to me as she leans her large body against mine.

We feel so intimately connected, and after a few moments, she makes the most loving, joyful tones, which deeply move me. I lay my face against her smooth skin, consumed by her welcoming energy. She immediately wriggles from my arms and swims away. "Oh, no, too close. Smothering," I think.

But she returns, jumping out of the water to give me a kiss by putting her rostrum (bottlenose) to my cheek. She swims around quickly and comes back again, offering me her pectoral fins, which I take in my own hands. Together we sway back and forth in our own sort of dance, and she doesn't even seem to mind when I inadvertently step on the tip of her tail. Again I receive a sweet kiss and she swims quickly away, only to return once again, curling her tail fully underneath her and rising up out of the three-and-a-half feet of water that we are in to literally stand right in front of me. She opens her pectoral fins wide and leans forward until her body touches mine, closing her fins around me in an enormous embrace. My dear dolphin friend sings with the most joyful tones, and these tones physically vibrate through my body.

"Breathe. Stay in your body. Where's it going? Feel it!"

I find myself immediately in an altered state, and yet my body-worker mentality keeps me present to the experience. I realize that there is no place within me that these tones are not vibrating; they are in each and every one of my cells. These luscious tones move through me with an intense clearing force. There is an especially strong pressure in my heart, causing it to ache deeply.

I witness an explosion of dark matter within me, bursting in every direction as something indefinable is released from my heart center. Heavy, dark debris clears, releasing its stifling hold. I continue to tell myself to consciously keep breathing, as I am completely overwhelmed. I hear the others murmur in the background, and their voices help to keep me present.

Intuitively I am moved to look up, and I see that just a foot or so from my head,

there is a massive, dark eye staring deeply at and into me. Exposed, dismantled
from the darkness of the burdens of my heart, and embraced by this massive, yet
truly gentle creature, I feel as if I am being authentically seen! We have the
deepest and sweetest connection, and then, moments later, she suddenly opens
her fins and releases me, and she is gone.

I sank down into the warm water as an enormous grin overtook my face. It remained there for a very long time, and my body vibrated with an unusual resonance for days. Unlike the usual clicks and whistles that dolphins make, Amaya sang to me in melodic, rich tones similar to what you might encounter with whales. Those remarkable sounds penetrated the emotional and energetic armor surrounding my heart, seemingly there to protect it, but in effect closing it off from the ability to experience and feel joy. Avoiding feeling my emotional pain had also clogged the channels for feeling positive emotions, too.

I openly rejected the label of "victim" for years, refusing to let the harshness of my childhood define who I was as an adult. This stance served me in that it helped to create an outer-focused steam that catapulted me onward with a desire for achievement and success. However, I now realize that I was not understanding that whether I actually spoke the word or not— having been a victim *did define* me. The reality of its hold on me was demonstrated in subtle ways, like the huge fear I experienced in relationships that left me vulnerable, or the terror I felt when outer experiences triggered inner memories. Still, life continued to support my soul evolution in spite of my not wanting to admit to being a victim. I observed outer symbols that reflected inner struggles and personal triumphs, indisputable signs to let me know I was on the right track! One such example appeared during my first shallow dive at Manchones Reef on Isla Mujeras.

The drone of the motor offers a meditation of sorts as our boat gently cuts across
the stunning aquamarine, teal, and cobalt blue Caribbean water. I find this water
to be the most healing of any I've ever been in, as the warm temperature and

heavy salt content cradle my body in womb-like buoyancy. I love it here! And surely, it is a beautiful Caribbean morning!

As we arrive at our dive destination, the meditative sound of the motor peters out. The others quickly gather their gear, dropping backwards into the warm water and disappearing beneath the surface. I dawdle, trying to deal with an overwhelming sense of anxiety. The weight of the equipment on my body literally takes my breath away. I feel as if I am pinned by an unknown, unwanted force that sucks the life air right out of me.

Jesus (Hey-Zeus), our guide, is already in the water, trying to coax me in. I have known him for some time, arranging for others on my trips to go off on adventures with him, but never before participating myself.

"It'll be all right, amiga, jump in. I will be here with you."

"I can't. I don't know why . . . I . . . I . . . I just . . . can't breathe," I say between shallow, forced, and quite desperate breaths. I sit poised backwards on the edge of the boat, unable to move either backwards into the water or forward into the boat. I am literally frozen with fear.

Jesus becomes still. All I can hear are the waves hitting against the boat as I rock back and forth with the motion of their impact.

"Doe-na, right now, in this moment, all over the world, people are wishing they were in the Caribbean . . . .

YOU . . . are here."

Plunk. I drop backwards into the water, immediately feeling a strong hand gently grasp mine. Jesus beams at me through his mask, encouraging me by giving a universal thumbs-up with his free hand. Together we swim downward into the depths. The others are not within sight. All around us, the magnificent Caribbean holds me in the warmth of her blessed womb. In the distance, under the water, I see the outline of something that looks familiar, yet displaced: it is a huge stone cross. Jesus leads me down, down, down, toward the cross. I am no longer terrified; newfound fascination draws me to the cross.

When we arrive, Jesus gives me the OK sign, and when I nod, he releases my hand. As I relax into the audible sound of my own breath, taking in and releasing vital oxygen through the dive equipment, I circle the cross. I find the sound of my own breath comforting. A delicate cut-out in the stone leaves a space, insinuating Christ's nailed body upon the cross. Multi-colored tropical fish, including angel fish, swim around us and through the empty cut-out . . . .

Barracuda, too, hover nearby. We have been warned not to wear anything shiny, as they are attracted to the sparkle. People, too, are attracted to what sparkles. Young ones possess a vibrant life force, and sometimes "barracudas" of all shapes and forms are attracted to the shiny new lights.

. . . Jesus once again asks if I am OK, and then he lets me surface on my own. Once settled into the boat, I feel great exhilaration.

My first dive took me unexpectedly back to the looming image of the cross. This time, instead of being surrounded by angry red flames that seemed impenetrable, the cross was submerged in boldly blue water that appeared welcoming and accepting. The significance of my fear around falling backwards into the unknown, the irrational weight of the equipment on my chest, the synchronicity of being supported by Jesus (Hey-Zeus), and the complete surprise of the cross at the bottom of the bay were collaborative events that brought me deeper, deeper into my own wounding. A further curiosity was discovered when Jesus spoke to me of his early desire to become a priest, having entered the seminary as a younger man for a short time. His still-devout faith was the energy offered by the hand that led me down to the submerged cross. A strong symbol of both the surface of the unconscious and the emotional body, the water's edge demanded that I encounter my fear as I was asked to "fall backwards" into the watery surface. Diving beneath the water, I found a strange vision in that beautiful tropical setting, and in seeing those colorful, life-affirming angel fish swimming inside the cross, I encountered an external symbol for my internal healing process.

One of the core premises of Depth Psychology[41] is Carl Jung's concept of the *transcendent function*. Central to the idea of individuation (self-becoming), the transcendent function allows us to move beyond the dichotomy of the conscious and the unconscious, the known and the hidden, the good and the evil. As we hold the tension of these opposites, we open to the gift of new insight, moving toward integrated wholeness.

On a recent trip back to this tropical island, I found that not far from the still-present cross, new artistic additions had been placed by Jason de Caires Taylor, a diver and ecologist. Underwater sculptures come to life as the sea growth they are designed to cultivate forms around them. Demonstrating a hopeful harmony between nature and culture, these statues of men and women depict an intricate village of sorts, resting on the sandy bottom. The underwater museum (MUSA)[42] draws tourists away from the endangered natural reef, assuring the natural Mother her privacy as she tries to regenerate her threatened waters. I found one especially touching and symbolic form of a big-bellied, pregnant woman. Mesmerizing, her soulful eyes provide a distinctly hopeful sign for what might be newly birthed from the depths of my own, as well as our collective, unconscious.

Ceremonial Blue Bowl: an old paradigm shatters

Many spiritual teachers speak about a breaking point that precedes significant growth, and although I have long since encountered what I believe to have been my *dark night of the soul*, during the writing of this manuscript one of my ceremonial bowls literally shattered. The crystal glass bowl had been a gift from a friend—an old-fashioned salad bowl that I often used to symbolically hold water during a cleansing or a release ceremony. Its deep vibrant color, the same natural blue as ocean water, was remarkably gorgeous.

When I placed the bowl (for the first time ever) gently on top of my treatment table, this vivid crystal blue bowl unexpectedly *exploded* with a deep, loud "pop," sending shards of glass in all directions.[43] Moments before, the bowl had been gracefully cradled within my arms. I was gratefully relieved to notice that I was physically unscathed, even though the force and reverberation of the explosion were close enough to have physically shaken me.

During earlier times of abuse, my psychic path of escape came from turning my awareness away from the physical reality I was experiencing and toward a line of candles on the altar. For some unknown reason, I was always attracted to the ones cradled in the cobalt-blue containers (never the red), as I moved with my awareness into the comforting light of their bright flames. Could the force of the bowl shattering be symbolic of the disintegration of the old paradigm of my having to avoid the reality of the abuse? Could it have shattered any false safety found in keeping this horrible secret, instead opening my personal pieces to be scattered far and wide?

Acknowledging the Victim

I now realize that my heroic, victim-renouncing stance, although practical and productive, left a wounded part of me behind. Unless I acknowledge and heal her, the betrayal of an innocent child remains within me; and even if I choose to reject that aspect of myself, her influence remains as I mature.

What comes to mind when you hear the word "victim?" I always thought of that word in a particular way; yet, in preparation for writing this narrative, I researched its actual definition and was shocked by what I found. The Merriam-Webster dictionary defines victim first and foremost as, "a living being sacrificed to a deity or in the performance of a religious rite."[44] When I look at it that way, I realize that I am, without a doubt, in the *shadow of truth*, a victim. Plain and simple, there it is—I am a victim.

Victims don't have just one face: the stereotypical weak and helpless one. Strong survivors can be victims, too. Definitely there are many of us who not only survive, but also thrive—with a vengeance. Overachievers, driven by a compulsion for success, may be responding to those who hurt them with an "I'll show you" attitude!

But what about the child within who is still hurt? She is in there, somewhere, with her aching heart. What we push away from us has a way of acting out like an angry child. Years ago, when I first encountered my wounded inner child, she glared at me with rage in her eyes and said, "It is YOU who kept me captive all these years!" It seemed that she had all but forgotten about the abuse by the perpetrators. My inability to embrace her wounding had kept her under lock and key. Matthew Fox writes about this important aspect of self-forgiveness in *Original Blessing*:

> The purpose of self-forgiveness is to shine light on the illusions, fears, and self-judgments that have held us captive in the role as our own jailer . . . . Self-forgiveness is a quiet birth. It is inherent in those moments when the compassion, love, and glory of the greater Self [are] born within our direct experience and known beyond old definitions.[45]

Acknowledging the victim and embracing her opens the door to moving beyond subtle victim patterns to true healing. Looking in the face of her ugliness conveys our sincere regard for what she endured and serves as a unifying force. I now draw that young victim to my own adult breast, comforting her and hoping that from here forward, I will never again abandon her, but will instead carry her close to my heart—always. It's the very least I can do.

Why I Am Writing

In the presence of the Heart Center, I also need to articulate that this exploration is not meant to be an attack on the Catholic Church, but rather a portrayal of my memories of abuse and the healing that followed. After my ardent research, I wrote an academic profile merging volumes of information, and that first effort informs this exploration. I wholeheartedly appreciate these expert trailblazers, who have exposed a cycle of abuse that has existed for centuries. Having memories that include oral, vaginal, and anal penetration in bizarre and twisted rituals on the church altar, and in other makeshift areas, leads me to believe that much that we have publically heard about these incidents is only the tip of the iceberg of what existed. Yet, I was shocked—and at the same time relieved—to read outrageously bizarre accounts, similar to those that I remembered, being voiced by others before me.

Amy Berg, the editor/producer of the ground-breaking and Academy Award-nominated documentary, *Deliver Us From Evil: Innocence and Faith Betrayed*, says, "to tell your story saves your soul, but also saves our soul to hear it." This 2006 film documents both a 1600-year-old cover-up by the Roman Catholic Church regarding pedophilia (child sexual abuse) and the story of one particular priest, Father Oliver O'Grady. The one who protected Fr. Oliver, Cardinal Roger Mahoney, was at the time of the release of this documentary "still in office fighting sexual allegations against 556 priests in his diocese." He retired in 2011, but he continues to be visible with a blog entitled, *Personal Reflections and Experiences from the Archbishop Emeritus of Los Angeles.*

Deliver Us from Evil reports that

> Pope Benedict XVI was accused of conspiracy to cover up sexual abuse in the United States. At the Vatican's request, President Bush granted the Pope immunity from prosecution. Since 1950, sexual abuse has cost the church over 1 billion dollars in legal settlements and expenses. Over 100,000 victims of clergy sexual abuse have come forward in the United States alone. Experts say more than 80% of sexual abuse victims never report their abuse.[46]

To speak about these memories has been scary, and to write about them terrifying. I know that there are many who will not believe me, some who will challenge me, and a few who will blame me. Why in the world would I make something like this up? What would I have to gain? If I was merely seeking to weave a story, I would choose a much more interesting and delightful one. I would be the beneficiary of great goodness! My initial initiation would bring me to a land of fairies, white horses, princesses, and flowers of every shape and hue; days would be spent with all the ice cream a little girl could eat! Not this. Why would I *choose* this?

Honestly, there were times when I doubted myself, questioning the strength of my memory. There were times when I wondered how in the world this outrageous behavior could have been done by those supposedly "holy" leaders. There were times when I was shocked that anyone could actually get away with such things. In those moments of contemplation and doubt, the perfection of life itself brought to me the exact right experiences to point out the strange logic of it all and to confirm the validity of all that I remembered.

The Heart Chakra for Healing

The act of one's own suffering (the wound), how you endure that wound, and ultimately how you transform it (healing), all have meaning and purpose (Key #3). Every piece of the healing process counts. Healing does not usually occur in one magical moment (although it *is* possible), but normally happens over time and space in a constantly shifting and reorganizing energetic field. The power of your wound, and the enormity of the pain you have felt, is an indication of the potential for you to transform.

We find a clue to the opportunity given in the 4th Key to Wholeness by returning to the Wounded Healer archetype described in Key #3. This concept was inspired by the mythology of the Greek god, Chiron, who eternally sought healing for his personal wound. This ancient myth was also the inspiration for the naming of a relatively newly discovered planet, Chiron, considered to be the "rainbow bridge between the inner and the outer planets." International astrological authority, Barbara Hand Clow, claims that Chiron can either be a killer or a healer, because it rules our initiation into the next level of our awareness, the next level necessary for our development. She says, "Chiron is alchemist and healer, initiator and visionary, teacher of integrity and bravery."[47] When we consider the cosmos as the macrocosm and each of us, individually, as the microcosm, it is fascinating to ponder Barbara's encouraging words.

The Wounded Healer lives in your heart, the bridge of the chakra system, as the connecting point between the lower (physical) chakras and the upper (spiritual) ones. Your innermost heart harbors the victim, keeping her safe until you can fully embrace her in your own right time. The 4th Key to Wholeness is found by turning love inward, so you can heal the pain. Love is the ultimate healing key; your own love and acceptance are remarkably potent healing agents. Although no one escapes trauma completely unmarked, a healed wound can become a beautiful testimony to resiliency and survival.

An integrated woman is one who accepts herself—scars and all. She may be a woman who is still in the process of healing, as she learns to know, accept, and love herself on all levels: mind, body, and spirit. The wound itself may hold a combination of our greatest dread and our greatest gifts. Claim your role as a Wounded Healer who utilizes the trauma and the challenges you have faced for the higher good—for your personal evolution, for your family and community, and ultimately, for all of us.

Let your Wound become your Strength.

Moving from Fear to Love

> Our doubts are traitors, and make us lose the good we oft might win,
>
> by fearing to attempt.
>
> ~ William Shakespeare

Opening to love is one of our greatest human challenges! Greeting vulnerability and learning trust are not easy tasks, ones that are especially difficult when you've been betrayed and hurt at a young age. But some of the most precious parts of life involve our connection with other people. We must somehow find a way to comfort our hearts and at the same time, try to let someone else in. To complicate matters, the path of heart is most often non-linear. It does not progress step-by-step toward a designated goal, but instead involves a lot of back and forth, one step forward and two or three back—then, you dash ahead only to be left behind. Through all of its twists and turns, it is a path worth taking . . . .

Paradoxically, it can also be through the letting go of relationships that do not serve us, but rather reinforce negative or destructive patterns, that we learn meaningful lessons of love and intimacy. By letting go of another, we can reinforce our respect for ourselves. We may even more fully get to know ourselves after letting go of a destructive or dysfunctional relationship, one in which we have been "giving ourselves away." Derek Walcott speaks of *Love after Love*:

> The time will come
> when, with elation,
> you will greet yourself arriving
> at your own door, in your mirror,
> and each will smile at the other's welcome,
>
> and say, sit here. Eat.
> You will love again the stranger who was your self.
> Give wine. Give bread. Give back your heart
> to itself, to the stranger who has loved you
>
> all your life, whom you ignored
> for another, who knows you by heart.
> Take down the love letters from the bookshelf,
>
> the photographs, the desperate notes,
> peel your own image from the mirror.
> Sit. Feast on your life.[48]

Cutting the Cords that Bind Us

Even though our trauma most likely originated outside of us, perpetuating the wound is sometimes an inside job. We can remain locked into negative patterns of abuse by attracting people who do horrible things, reminiscent of the original abuse. This sounds crazy, but when the pattern is familiar, it may feel comfortable even though it hurts. And those who reject obvious patterns of abuse may still have negative nuances of limitation caused by an underlying sense of not deserving or a feeling of being tainted by the past.

Codependency occurs when we are so enmeshed with another person or an experience that our very survival is dependent upon that person or experience. Our moods are affected by the other person and our ability to cope with life is greatly influenced by what the person does or does not do. *Independency* is being completely free from any bonds, acting solely through the influence of our own merits and our own foibles. Like Goldilocks sitting in chairs in the bears' cottage, codependence swallows us by keeping us hidden within its huge boundaries, while being totally independent is like not being able to rest at all. Not only are we not sitting in anyone's chair, but frankly, we aren't even in the cabin. We are out in the huge world all by ourselves. *Interdependency* is the ability to meet and navigate through life with a desire and capacity to connect and disconnect, as appropriate, without becoming absorbed with another. We have our independence and our connection, too. Interdependency is like sliding into that one perfect seat and finding it "Just Right!"

Learning to cut the cords and tendrils that bind you is one way to shift from codependency to interdependency. Begin by finding a time that you can have privacy without interruption. Sit in a quiet room in a comfortable chair. If it helps you to have a journal and pen in your lap to record any observations and your immediate thoughts after this process, then go ahead and do so. It is also not necessary for the success of this particular process to write about it.

- Begin by reflecting on who you are—the quality and aspects of your character.
- Contemplate your life experiences, and notice if there is a strong tug or a sense of being tied to one or more parts of your past.
- Some people are so aware of these ties that they can literally "see" them. If you cannot, just open to the sense of noticing if it "feels" as if there is something there. Turning your attention toward it will encourage it to make itself known to you. We are not trying to make a mountain out of a molehill here; we are simply turning to look in

each direction, so we can see the mountain that has been there the whole time.

- If you identify such a cord tying you to your past, make gentle contact with it. Do not tug on it or try to break it. Touch it gently and let it know you are there. Approach it with a stance of acceptance rather than aggression.

- Open to consider any benefit that you may have received from remaining connected with this person or this situation. Sometimes this is a bit of a stretch: for example, "by keeping connected with this event, I have avoided taking risks, which has given me a sense of safety." Or, "Steven has kept me dependent on his money for my daily survival, so I haven't had to work."

- Then, explore the opportunity for advancement that might emerge if you let go of your limiting connection with the old way. "Even though it feels safe, not taking risks has limited my ability to try. I want to experiment in new ways, taking the chance of failure in order to see success." Or, "I want to experience a greater sense of purpose to my life. Even though it is scary, I want to be responsible for my own financial support."

- Go back and forth between looking at how this cord has served you and looking at how releasing it will help you to grow. Keep going back and forth with this comparison until you feel complete.

- Then, thank the cord for keeping you in touch with what has served you in some way. Kindly state that the time has come to let the old way go and to shift into a new way.

- Imagine a razor sharp, shiny blade easily and cleanly slicing through the cord or tendril, and see it fall into two pieces. It is important to imagine a finely sharpened blade so it will be a clean break. As soon as you make the cut, the piece connected to you shrivels and turns to a darkened color. The life force has literally gone out of it, and in a very short time (usually a second or two), it falls off, releasing any hold on you.

- Recognize and give thanks for your own ability and power, fed by the 3rd and the 4th chakras.

- Know that you hold a personal responsibility to move beyond bitterness and blame. Take steps to release the ties that bind you to the past or to a dysfunctional present. Create change!
- Step out in your life in a way that is in alignment with the release of this cord. To cut a cord without re-patterning your behavior causes a new tendril to emerge, recreating a similar "new" cord. Treat the wound by moving into a fresh pattern. Practice emotional and behavioral alignment with the new reality you wish to live as your own.

4th Key to Wholeness: the survivor embraces the victim

Knowing that an effective way to escape our personal struggles is by courageously navigating through them provides hope-filled encouragement, urging us onward, regardless of how difficult our process of healing may be. The 8 Keys and their prospective doorways open into a vast and transcendent potential within us, one that conveys the value of moving beyond our wounds and the reality that we can, in fact, accomplish the task of healing. The 8 Keys also hold a rich promise for what can be mined through our efforts. We can pattern or re-pattern both our personality and our outer life expression to embrace so much more of what is possible within us! In *The Naked Sword*, John R. Haule says that "our inner nature has been seeking us all along,"[49] and Alexis De Tocqueville wrote

> I need not traverse earth and sky
> to discover a wondrous object woven of contrasts,
> of infinite greatness and littleness, of intense gloom and amazing brightness,
> capable at once of exciting pity, admiration, terror, contempt.
> I have only to look at myself.[50]

Take a close look at yourself now. What parts of you remain stuck in your past? What wounds lie dormant within you, still painfully raw? Do you shun your vulnerable self—the one who was hurt? Are there resentments or feelings of bitterness that eat away at your insides? Soul retrieval allows you to go back and pick up what you have abandoned and integrate those pieces back into yourself. You have the power to put the golden key into the rusty lock and turn until it clicks. Reclaim those innermost orphans, so they can help you live in the fullness of who you truly are.

How Heavy is your Emotional Load?

It is also important to take the time to consider if you, in fact, have been energetically kidnapped—how much does your past experience affect your present reality? Are you stuck in a repetitive pattern or patterns that replay over and over? Does the past overshadow the opportunities of your present?

And what emotions have outlived their usefulness? When first wounded, it is normal to have reactive emotions, and quite healthy to develop through those emotions. Months or even years later, hanging onto bitterness, resentment, or a deep, deep sadness can be too heavy a burden to bear. Sit with the imagery of this little story and consider whether you, too, have lugged around your own version of a "woven basket" for way too long.

> There was a woman . . . who had a woven basket—it was simple in its shape and form, and it was a very sturdy container. In this basket, the woman placed her disappointments, her resentments, and her bitterness. In this basket, the woman placed her wounds. She held the basket tightly to her, guarding its contents, unknowingly believing them to be special and unique. In spite of their weight, they were very precious to her . . . .

> And so the woman carried her basket with her *everywhere*, clinging to it as she cradled it in her arms. Her disappointments, her resentments, her wounds, and her bitterness were not shared with others . . . or so the woman thought! When she spoke with her neighbor across the fence or bent down at the market to select her vegetables, some of the contents of the basket unwillingly spilled out, polluting the air around her with their rotting stench.

> Still, the woman clung to her basket, adding to it from time to time, until the

99

woman grew very, very old. The weight of the basket became too much to bear. The very old woman sat down under a tree with the basket huddled next to her, clinging to its rim.

A young boy came down the path and saw the old woman there, under the tree. He also saw her basket, which was very odd, for in all these years no one had actually seen the basket, even though it was there with her always. The young boy peered into the basket, struck by the weight of all that was inside.

"Grandmother, why do you keep all that rotting stuff?" he asked.

"I don't know," the woman replied honestly.

Together, they hoisted the basket full of its heavy contents, carefully turning it over at the nearby river's edge. Into the river tumbled the woman's disappointments, her resentments, her wounds, and her bitterness. The old woman watched as they moved away from her, down the river. She watched until they were out of sight, and she felt a little strange because they had been so much a part of her.

The little boy smiled, for he knew more than he could say to this old woman. Together they took the path homeward, the now empty basket swinging between them.[51]

The Path of Heart

My Native American teachers instruct that the greatest and often longest journey we make is from the head to the heart, being called to become vulnerable to one another and to life itself. On the difficult head-to-heart trek, we can also learn to love what is still vulnerable within ourselves or that part within us that was taken advantage of and wounded because of its innocence. Love is being present with what "is" and loving it anyway—and that includes the whole truth about who we are, where we have been, and what we have endured.

Throughout life's harsh suffering, it is easy to fall back on the dependable mind that judges, categorizes, and keeps us stuck in a limited stance of what we believe to be true. In all fairness, we must also acknowledge useful survival and coping mechanisms that are available to us through our minds. Still for some of us, the very thought of our wounding can make us cringe—as if hands could reach across space and time and the abusers could still "get" us. Visualizations such as "cutting the cords" can have concrete results in helping to free us from some of the energetic tendrils of some of those psychological bonds.

The brutality of abuse we may experience can often fall outside of rational reason. It is difficult to imagine why anyone would want to do those things, or why they *would* do those things to us. In the overall scheme, however, if we season our survival instinct and our logical intelligence with the sophisticated nuances of the heart, we can release the rigid filters of "right" and "wrong" and open to non-dualistic reasoning, which offers the possibility of so much more. In the expansiveness of the Heart chakra, compassion can be discovered, and forgiveness may be possible in even the worst of situations.

Again, we want to separate the idea of forgiveness from condoning abuse or in any way implying that wounding perpetuated by one person onto another is acceptable. Forgiveness is a highly charged and complex facet of healing, one that cannot possibly be given the space it deserves here. When it comes to the things that deeply hurt us, both natural occurrences (like tornadoes) and those perpetrated by other people (like sexual abuse), sometimes there just aren't logical explanations for why these things happened or any excuse for them to have happened at all.

Embracing Yourself

- Initially, just entertain the idea that the limited, black-and-white reaction to your wounding can be replaced with a multi-colored understanding possessing a wider variance, rich in nuances of subtle insight.
- Forgiveness may start with the complex process of accepting the reality of whatever horrible trauma has happened; by recognizing your wounds, their transformation begins.
- Often one of the most pivotal steps is found in forgiving yourself because the receiver of the abuse often blames herself for what happened to her, regardless of her age at the time these things occurred.

- Take some time to sit in a quiet space with your journal and a pen to capture your thoughts.

- Create a list of what you know about your wounding. Include your age, the circumstance, and any details you think may be important to the overall picture.

- You do not need to rehash the whole thing in detail. Just create a brief list to set down a clear capsule of what happened.

- If your wounding happened as a child, you may want to retrieve a photo of yourself at the age of your trauma. It may be remarkable to see how young you were at the time.

- Now just sit there with those pieces of information. Look at them logically. Notice any "ahas" that come to you in the moment.

- Also examine your list through the fine filter of your heart. Be present with your emotions, regardless of what emotions arise. What do you feel? Anger/rage? Sadness? Terror? Relief? Or even no emotion at all? Record whatever you notice about what you are feeling right now as you revisit those details. (Need I say it. There is no right or wrong answer with any part of this process).

- Now open to the emotions of your heart, as you honestly evaluate the circumstances of your situation. Whether you were a child or an adult when the wounding occurred, what, if anything, could you have done to make it different? Be careful of considering "what ifs" that just weren't a part of your reality at the time. For example, "what if I ran away?" or "what if I didn't go to that party?" are paths that lead nowhere, because honestly we can never know these answers.

- On the other hand, if you consider your situation from the point of view of what was realistically within your control, it may be easier to come to terms with your part in it.

- The bottom line is that the abuse or trauma has happened, and nothing you can ever do will change it.

- What is in your power, right here and right now, is to recognize that hurt part or parts of you. And to take her in your arms and love her. No matter what.

- No amount of love from the outside in will ever be enough to fill that aching space. You are the one that must fill the gaping hole with your own acceptance and your own love.

- Sometimes it may seem that if you love the vulnerable parts of yourself, it will perpetuate them, but in fact, loving them enables them to heal and grow strong. Loving them enables them to transform into something much better.

- At the end of your contemplation, send yourself love. You can close your eyes and imagine the warmth of your own love and acceptance surrounding you like a nurturing and cozy blanket.

- You might even wrap your arms around you, stretching across your body from shoulder to shoulder. Or perhaps you can hold your face in your own hands . . . and know that "she" will never be completely alone. Even if everyone around her disappoints or abandons her, she will never be alone if you can stand by her in the horror of the truth of what happened and not push her away.

- Then, perhaps someday, you can truly forgive her. Because it was not her fault.

Have you caught a glimmer of yourself in these pages? Have you seen a meaning that resonates with your own healing? I know that within your journey of healing, there is the ability to discover so much more of your truest being. On the Path of Heart, we are asked again and again to try to see the bigger picture. We are asked again and again to forgive and to trust ourselves. We are asked again and again to trust in love.

You deserve to experience the beauty and the richness of love, in spite of how that might make you feel vulnerable. Let love rise up in you; be an expression of love. That connection with your own love and allowing its fluid expression, more than anything will pave the way for love to come to you, through others and through all the channels of your life. Step through the now-open doorway of the 4th Key to Wholeness: as the survivor embraces the victim, you choose the Path of Heart.

Breathe slowly, in and out, for three or four breath cycles. Imagine the red ray of the first power center grounding you, the orange ray of the second power center stimulating your creative ability to manifest wellness, and the yellow ray from your third center bringing meaning and purpose to every facet of your life. Now, imagine the green hue of your heart center flowing easily and gracefully through all parts of you, as you speak with assurance the following affirmative blessing:

In the comforting flow of the Heart Chakra, I am able, once and for all, to embrace my victim self, to draw her to my breast, and to accept her in all her facets, knowing that truly, she is a part of me. I breathe easily and fully into the nurturing warmth of the heart center, taking in vital life force energy for every part of my body and soul. I anticipate the good that comes my way today, as I relax into the Divine Flow, knowing my life has meaning and purpose. I commit myself to learning to give and receive love from a place of appropriate vulnerability balaced with true connection. I now embrace love. As I open further to the Path of Heart, I season my words and actions with my own heart essence and marvel at life's transformative adventure. My life unfolds anew in remarkable ways! I am healthy, vibrant, and fully engaged in the wonder of my life.

5th Key

Breaking the Silence
to Speak Our Truth

If you bring forth what is within you,

what you bring forth will save you.

If you do not bring forth what is within you,

what you do not bring forth will destroy you.

~ Jesus Christ, Gospel of Thomas (50 AD)

The *Vishuddha* or Throat Chakra provides me with a Voice. Speaking is a precious gift that enables me to communicate my thoughts, my needs, and my desires. Even the unspoken word, captured in writing, is fed by the energy of this 5th chakra. I celebrate this powerful tool by speaking my honest truth, and I am heard in the integrity of my words. In the same manner, I also honor others with attentive listening and understanding. My communication is clear and holds meaning.

Have you ever noticed skewed or distorted communication that somehow misses the mark in conveying the intended meaning? There are times when we don't know how to formulate what we want to say; other times when we do our best, but our meaning is still misunderstood; and still other times when we engage in what might be considered mindless chatter! For some of us, speaking our innermost thoughts may be something we have never done, don't know how to do, or are afraid to do. Communication is not only a skill, but also a blessed human right found through the 5th Key to Wholeness.

Our Throat Chakra helps us to develop the ways and the means for clear communication through the spoken and written word, and even seasons our subtler forms of communication, such as body language and facial expressions. Turning this 5th Key to unlock our throat center enables us to access our lost or unspoken words and the emotions connected with them, lending healing energy to the old wounds and releasing understanding for the unresolved parts of ourselves. Breaking the silence to speak our truth taps into the power of the 5th Chakra and in turn, the 5th Chakra, offers healing and empowerment by providing energy that can help us overcome our fearful silence.

Keeping Horrible Secrets

As children, abuse victims are often instructed by the perpetrator not to "tell," and as adults we may continue to hold in the strictest confidence the details of what happened to us, or even the fact that it happened at all. Thus, a lasting burden of childhood abuse often lies in keeping its secrets.

I have understandable concerns when I think of sharing this information. It is difficult to hear. It is difficult to know. One girlfriend broke down in uncontrollable sobs when I shared my memories; another went to the rest room and vomited; and a man I had been dating for several months (a former Catholic altar boy) started having heart palpitations. I had to calm *him* down. Many people just aren't equipped psychologically or emotionally to handle this kind of information, and because it happened so long ago, there is nothing anyone can do to change it anyway; even the held knowledge of it may become stuck energy with no apparent productive path of expression.

Abused children often ask, when they grow into adults, how come no one knew what was happening to them. Why didn't someone see what was wrong? Why didn't someone come to help? Even the brightest, most well-adjusted child does not necessarily have the capacity to verbalize the horrors of sexual abuse while it is happening to her. And even if she did, the adults around her may be so conditioned by societal taboos that they are often blind to the potential for the reality about which I am speaking. We don't want to think about it, we don't want to talk about it, and we don't want to believe it happens.

When I was eleven, I moved from the only city I had known to a fresh new town with grass and trees and more space to stretch. I changed from a parochial to a public school and left the abuse behind me. Although the transition was difficult in many ways, there was a newly found freedom in public schools, as teachers were more open, engaging students in thought-provoking discussion rather than simply instructing them in doctrine. Things within me began to shift, too. Within a month or two, I awoke one morning unable to close my mouth.

It hurts to swallow, and it even hurts to breathe through my mouth. I can't possibly close my mouth because of the large, swollen mass encompassing my mouth, my jaw, and my throat. My parents take me to our pediatrician, thinking that I might have the mumps; he shakes his head and refers me to the dentist. At Dr. Dean's, my mouth is stretched wide: "Yow-ch!" After a very thorough examination, he sprays several different kinds of liquid into my mouth and down my throat.

The pain and the swelling continue for a number of days, and nothing seems to ease its intensity; finally, my father suggests salt water rinses. The warm water and potent salt of these rinses sooth the angry fire and biting soreness in my mouth and throat, effectively drawing out the poison.

The dentist diagnoses this strange outbreak as herpes.

Body wisdom knew how to speak even when I did not, and body wisdom also knew it was time to purge the great irritation. Even though the words could not yet be spoken out loud, at eleven, I no longer needed to hold the full toxicity of this horrible secret. Beloved Louise Hay, a well-known authority on reading physical symptoms for their emotional and spiritual content, shares in her international best-selling book, *You Can Heal Your Life*, that herpes reflects a "mass belief in sexual guilt and the need for punishment. Public shame. Belief in a punishing God."[52] Rather than the prescribed medicated washes, the cleansing and neutralizing power of salt water rinses brought relief for this imbalance. It's interesting to note that the treatment that finally soothed and healed the systemic rash that spontaneously erupted while I was writing this manuscript involved a couple of trips to the Indian Hot Springs, which are rich in natural salts.

The process of cleansing my mouth and throat continued over several decades. Many layers of blockages were cleared, by necessity, in order to open the channel of my individual voice. The development of my professional work was tightly entwined with the need and the ability to speak my personal truth. In the fall of 1991, I held the first of what would be many retreats over the next eighteen years. A year or two later, my mother flew in from Connecticut to join a full group of 47 people for our annual Pathweavers Retreat in Grand Lake, Colorado.

On our drive into the mountains, my mother curiously asks how it's been having my father live with me, knowing that the two of us often clashed when I was growing up—two strong wills hitting each other head-on and me, being the child, usually taking the brunt of our exchanges. With the warmth and caring of my mother so obvious in this moment, I find myself unexpectedly inclined to say something about the abuse. There is no good time to tell a parent such a thing. Mom already knows about my memories, but she doesn't know the exact details. She asks me point blank where this happened to me.

"Church," I say, bracing myself for her denying reaction.

Without pause, she responds immediately.

"Do you think it happened to your sister? Because I always thought something happened to your sister . . . ."

"I don't know."

My devout Catholic mother who I expect will argue with me or deny my memory then says, thoughtfully, "You used to disappear for long periods of time, and you were vague about where you were—up the street, or at the park."

I'm stunned, and I consciously try to keep myself present enough to keep the car on the road.

Mom continues after a few minutes, ". . . But I would have had to dress up three small children to go looking for you," she mumbles, mostly to herself.

We lived across the street from the church and the school. My mother's response told me that what I remembered was certainly possible. They had me six days a week during school and church, but they also had access to me even when I wasn't officially there.

Mom and I drove in silence the rest of the way, each immersed in our own thoughts as we navigated the mountain contours leading to the small town of Grand Lake. By the time we arrived, less than an hour later, my voice had already become strained, and as I taught a pre-program class, it disappeared altogether. I had a bad case of laryngitis . . . and a full retreat program to lead!

I called on the help of my trusted inner guides and Spirit, saying, "I know you haven't helped me to assemble all these people, plan a powerful program, and haul all of this stuff up the mountain, just to have me be unable to speak. *Do something!*"

I had hardly any voice above a whisper, a gravelly rumble, and an intermittent squeak until I took the microphone in my hand to welcome my guests. In a miraculous moment when I opened my mouth to begin, the power of my words returned. This experience demonstrated to me the intensity of the wounding held within my body and the reactive potential of forcing myself to speak about what I resisted acknowledging verbally. The marriage of body and emotions was to be tested many times over the next 22 years as I unwound the constrictive tendrils, reminiscent of a brutal and confusing time long-since past.

Vow of Silence

"Quiet—don't speak about these things." Whether it evokes a forced promise or conveys an unspoken threat, the abuser's message is typically clear: "tell and wrath will descend upon you (the victim), not me (the perpetrator)." Mary Gail Frawley-O'Dea, an expert on child abuse, says

> Some perpetrators overtly extract secrecy by suggesting that the victim will be blamed for the abuse, then taken from his or her home and placed in an orphanage. Or they threaten that if the victim discloses, the perpetrator will harm him or her or members of the family.[53]

I agreed not to speak out because threats were made about killing my sister—a common control tactic to elicit compliance. Although many years have passed and the logic of those threats has long since expired, it has been rare for me to share any part of these experiences. Through 27 years as a public speaker and spiritual teacher, and almost 40 years working in helping professions assisting others with their wounding, I held my own deep wounding inside me. In spite of having the ability to communicate in sophisticated ways, I rarely referred to my childhood trauma, and when doing so, I was general and vague in detail, hesitant to directly connect my abuse with a church context.

Recently I saw a client with whom I have met a few times for work-related issues. Early in our session, she began to cry. With tears that continued to flow for almost an hour, she spoke about being eight years old and being coaxed into her next-door neighbor's house. She had not spoken to anyone about this experience. Recently she had been thinking about all the ways this one day still affects her life, and now she wanted to address it directly with the hope that she could loosen its hold upon her. Unspoken wounds do not go away, but fester beneath the skin (and within the spirit) until they are tended to. So, why did I make an unconscious decision to keep silent, and why did I remain so for most of my lifetime?

Clerical Abuse Contains Complex Secrets

We must also question why the Church and so many of its followers deny allegations even when there is proof to the contrary. Mark D. Jordon, a professor of religion at Emory, Notre Dame, and other Catholic universities, a highly-trained historian of Christian thought, refers to this denial as "blind faith" in the clergy. Some believe in the authority of the Church to sort it all out, while others believe in eternal damnation if they cross the leaders of their church.

Another factor that greatly influences denial and sets priestly pedophilia apart from other kinds of child abuse is that Catholics are pre-conditioned from birth to believe in the priest's role of secrecy as it relates to rituals and sacred doctrines. Priests hold secret the path to God, acting as a sort of bridge—allowing some to pass and denying passage to others. Jordon cites a fifth-century theological writer, Dionysus, while addressing the issue of secrecy and priests, saying that

> Christian priests, as teachers and ritual celebrants, open the way of ascent. They mediate divine illumination into our darkness. They tend to the most important secrets. The hierarchies of their offices and rituals form the indispensable veil around the invisible.[54]

This passage warrants repetition and further consideration. As Jordon says, "the hierarchies of their offices" (the patriarchal ladder) and the "rituals" (sacraments, including, in my case, a forced and tainted communion ritual), form the "indispensable veil" (a necessary, valuable cover) around the "invisible" (God). The priest holds the veil in place, and he is the way to God! Or does he keep us separate from our God—beholding us to him, a human with human frailties?

Jordon says that holy secrets and hierarchical power are enmeshed, the former supporting the latter. The hierarchy of the priesthood has been built on secrets and the right to keep them. The free reign this provides for the Church fosters the potential for misuse. Jordon affirms that

> . . . more importantly, the core priestly secrets can endow other sorts of secrets in church with a sense of rightness and inviolability. Priests confuse the secrets they are supposed to keep. They can be misled, not least by hierarchical cultures, into believing that what holds true of some of their secrets must hold true for all . . . clericalism makes the mistake of reading all priestly secrets "up" into sacred mysteries.[55]

Thus priests conditioned to believe that their secret-keeping was in the best interest of God could fathom that whatever they held secret was for this higher good:

> The priest was a living secret, the agent or actor for an essential secret. Could there be any stronger container for hiding sexual crimes—especially from oneself? The priest is a sacred figure who is a vicar for the hiddenness and immunity of the divine. His ordination sacralizes not only his privilege, but his body. If that body should carry "disgusting" secrets, they can be sealed under the grandest secrecy. They can be locked up alongside the mystery of God—which no one can betray.[56]

In the 1950's and 60's, the religious context of keeping holy secrets set the template for an environment that held the very priest who abused children in the position of being the one who forgave all secrets and sins in the holy sacrament of confession. In our lifetime, gratefully, we are seeing some systems set in place to make it harder for these kinds of secrets to be buried within the ranks of the clergy—clerical accountability is being called forth.

Another confusing influence that perpetuates denial in ritual abuse is what is referred to as religious duress. Because of the priest's respected role in the church, the silence of the victim may be purchased through the idea that it is beyond the capacity of a devout believer's imagination that a priest

> would do or attempt something evil or wrong . . . . Religious duress is a real but very special kind of fear. The ultimate source of this fear is a belief in an unseen but all-powerful supreme being who requires obedience, without which the believer is punished.[57]

In addition to being considered pure and holy, the priests, bishops, and the pope are thought to have the ability to determine what is and what is not a sin, leading devout Catholics to question their own inner authority at times. Doyle, Sipe, and Wall quote *The Catechism of the Council of Trent* (1543 - 1545)

> . . . . bishops and priests being, as they are, God's interpreters and ambassadors, empowered in His name to teach mankind the divine law and the rules of conduct and holding, as they do, His place on earth, it is evident that no nobler function than theirs can be imagined. Justly therefore are they called not only angels, but even gods, because of the fact that they exercise in our midst the power and prerogatives of the immortal God . . . . For the power of consecrating and offering the body and blood of our Lord and of forgiving sins, which has been conferred on them, not only has nothing equal or like it on earth, but even surpasses human reason and understanding.[58]

These ambassadors and interpreters of God are often thought to be above reproach.

It was difficult for a child raised in the Catholic faith to imagine being raped by a priest even if I knew it happened. In addition to the strong religious influence I experienced six days a week, previous generations of my French Catholic family produced nuns and priests, and the good work of these generous people was highly valued within my family. Early on, I, myself, longed to be a nun. The effect of religious duress, in my case, was holding the two co-existing pieces of reality in my mind and my heart: what had happened to me and what could not possibly have happened. The memories of a brutal rape and subsequent ritual abuse were pushed down in my psyche and held there for many years. Although hidden, they still had their way with me, expressing through life experience, such as my rebellious gang activity as a teen, and in physical imbalances, such as severe migraines and painful endometriosis. Edward Edinger says, ". . . nothing is ever lost, not even the blood pact with the devil. Outwardly it is forgotten, but inwardly not at all."[59] The pact made in Jesus' name, with my child self as sacrifice, had the power to bind me.

Clearing the Throat

Over a period of six years facilitating spiritual retreats in Mexico, my voice opened further and cleared some of the old psychic debris. Feminine energy is very strong on Isla de Mujeras, the "Isle of Women," home of the temple of the ancient Goddess Ixchel. I often led meditations on the beach on this beautiful Caribbean island, basking in the energy of our healing circles and savoring the moist salt air, the penetrating rays of the sun, and the freshly-sweet and tender breezes. The island provided a nurturing womb for transformation. One trip I found particularly challenging, because the corrective dental braces on my teeth had left deep cuts and open sores, causing my mouth and throat to be swollen with the poison of infection.

> *I realize if this condition doesn't shift soon, I will have to go to the clinic for antibiotics. I dread the inevitable. My guides instruct me to retrieve the large, black tourmaline from my suitcase. This particular healing stone had clearly "asked" to come with me when I was packing. Sitting at the dining room table in my hotel suite, I close my eyes. A strong wind rattles the window, making a distinctive hum. I match its tone, as I am instructed to touch the black tourmaline to the left side of my face, swollen with infection. I open my mouth wide and allow the sound through, noticing radiant warmth that appears and then grows beneath the stone.*

A large circle of women, in strongly vibrant blouses and multi-colored skirts, appears in my mind's eye. They present themselves to me, inviting me into their circle. I enter, with respect, looking from one to another kind, loving face. The tone of the wind at the window in front of me changes, and I shift my tone to match it.

There is a warm fire in the center of the women's circle, and they draw me toward it. The stone beneath my hand rests on my swollen jaw, heating up even more. No further words are spoken by the women, but in their vibrant gaze, I understand a lot . . . . Feminine wisdom is not confined by the limitation of spoken language.

I continue to sing various tones, as I am directed to gather the negative energy of the infection into the black stone. After a time, I complete and lay the saturated stone before me on the table. The window is now still as the wind has calmed.

"That was the most beautiful sound I ever heard," Pat Baker, my roommate, says. I did not hear her enter, but evidently she had been watching me for quite some time. My friend exclaims with genuine surprise how the swelling has gone visibly down in my face and neck.

The guides give one last instruction: go soak the stone and my face in the salt of the Caribbean water just steps away from my room. The swelling continues to go down, and by the next morning it has disappeared completely.

My voice also found ways to open indirectly through body language and facial expression, by necessity, since I had to communicate with people who spoke a different language. The island provided some interesting interactions for someone who did not speak Spanish.

I greet the sun at Ixchel's temple on the easternmost point of the island—the first place of the rising sun. Offering a sacred pipe ceremony, I stand overlooking the water on a small and perilous cliff of rocks. Behind me is a stalactite and stalag-

mite meeting place with a small hole, barely allowing human passage between them. There is no way out except back through the small hole.

I hear a male voice behind me laughing and turn to see a man approaching me. He appears disheveled, perhaps having been up all night drinking, as he swings an open beer bottle dangling precariously at his side. I cradle my precious pipe in my arms, glancing at the sacred objects spread out on a rock in front of me. There is no place for me to go. The jagged rocks at the water's edge are far below me, and my usual path of exit is blocked by this stranger, who is still moving toward me.

In an unexpectedly bold stance, I hold up my right hand toward him, and with every part of myself distinctly present, I feel a burst of power as I shout a strong "NO!"

"GO BACK! Get AWAY from me," I shout, not knowing if he even understands English.

The man looks at me stunned for a moment and then, bursts out crying. He literally sobs with his big chest heaving up and down. I now realize just how young he looks. Another man (who I had not even noticed) quickly crawls back through the hole, followed by his rattled friend. They leave with voices raised in excited Spanish. I have no idea what they are saying to one another, but I realize that my being empowered from my morning ceremonial work, partnered with a focused intention to protect my sacred objects, was an amazingly powerful stance. The laser clarity of my "NO" had penetrated his drunken mischief.

Victim Holds a Key

So with such potential power in my woman voice, why would I continue to hold my childhood secret after all these years? It was as if an unseen force held my silence in place. Each time I spoke about the abuse was a major event requiring extraordinary effort, and at times, the fear surrounding it was immense and all-encompassing. Even with the practical skills I possessed as a trained professional and the coping mechanisms I knew so well as a healer and a coach, the enormity of it was a lot to bear.

Just the thought of speaking about my past could bring on a shortness of breath, as if the life force would literally be sucked out of me if I spoke another word. Extreme panic! And an irrational feeling that I would die, or worse yet, cease to exist as the being that I was— an eternal kind of "death." Each time these reactions surfaced I would work them through, allowing myself to feel the feelings, but not to wallow in them. I pushed myself to move on, to keep moving through the enormity of them. At the same time, I also had to acknowledge the physical reality feeding my fear, recognizing that there was some truth to it.

The validity of victim reports is often questioned even when there is concrete evidence proving that the reports are true, and the Catholic Church has been known to attack victims, even when the perpetrator admits to the abuse, because these disclosures question the pure sanctity of the priest and the Church itself. As recorded by Leon Festinger's Cognitive Dissonance Theory, when information puts into question one's strongly held belief, instead of allowing the truth of that information to cause doubts and weaken that belief, one's reaction may, in fact, be to strengthen the familiar belief rather than to trust the challenging facts. The abuse itself, in some cases, may even seal a victim's commitment to the Church. Festinger says, "The general principle seems to be, that people come to believe in and to love the things they have to suffer for."[60] The possibility of a cognitive dissonance reaction is especially relevant when abuse is shrouded in a religion that celebrates suffering "in the name of God," and an impressionable child is abused using His name.

Our minds are challenged with the difficulty of holding the presence of those two conflicting thoughts—what we know happened and what could not possibly have happened. When we are presented with a reality that is too harsh to believe, our mind literally goes "tilt." The easiest thing may be to believe that we are at fault, that we are to blame . . . or to doubt that it ever happened in the first place. The same is true for those who hear a child's report.

In a blog entitled, *Fighting Cognitive Dissonance and the Lies We Tell Ourselves*, Dr. John M. Grohol says

> When individuals are presented with an irresolvable controversy, cognitive dissonance will help them rectify the dilemma by aligning to that which is best or easiest to believe is true for them. People who have the greatest need for consistent and orderly righteousness are the most likely to fall into the effects of cognitive dissonance.[61]

The devoutly religious certainly fall into this category. The authors of *Sex, Priests, and Secret Codes*, Father Tom Doyle, A. W. Sipe, and Patrick J. Walls (a practicing priest and two former priests), are very aware of the charged nature of this topic. They acknowledge their concern about being blamed because they speak out about priestly pedophilia and the church's role in the abuse, and they also point out that the sexual abuse within the Church has a long-standing history. And Jordon says, "You can take the question as asking whether the abuse really was a secret. It looks, in fact, like a perfect example of the open secret— evident truth refused."[62]

When victims speak out, it may feel as if the difficult task of exposing their wound hasn't made much of a difference. My keeping silent afforded the safe and peaceful space in which to create a life's work of service, allowing for expression *from* the wounding, without being kept entrenched in it. I had to, by necessity—for my own healing—move away from the grips of it. I believe I also actively rejected being identified with the wounded (victim) because I would rather be thought of as one who worked for the healing.

Yet, as I shared in Key #4, I now sincerely believe that embracing that "victim" self is an important part of our healing process. One can never truly hide from the truth. Marion Woodman speaks of the grace of allowing one's process to unfold in its own time.

> Gradually the perception changes; gradually the intimations are constellated. The forty years or forty days are accomplished. Then it is the task of the ego to bring into daily reality what has been revealed in the desert, to bring the

treasure home. Bringing the inner and outer worlds into harmony is living one's destiny.[63]

Over the past few years, it has felt as if it was time to reveal myself. Perhaps I can speak for others who cannot. I know I possess the tools and life experience to do so, having developed an inner and outer network of support for this bold stance. And in a moment of still contemplation, I had a remarkable visual download in which I clearly saw that the priest's denial on the one hand was also held in place by the victim's silence. All things are ultimately connected, and each one of us who does not speak out contributes to the energetic see-saw that allows the perpetrator to go up as the victim goes down. Each time we hold the guilt, the shame, the regret, and the pain, we deny him the opportunity to rightly carry it for himself.

As I shift, my shift *does* affect others. Whether I speak truth in the privacy of my own home or shout it through a microphone to an auditorium full of people, my voice makes a difference. The experience on Ixchel's point, the easternmost tip of Mexico, demonstrated the strength of my voice when I am clearly aligned. That morning's first dawning light illuminated and confirmed my personal strength and personal power.

In any relationship, the most pliable element is that of our own behavior. I choose to no longer let my fears control me. I choose to be fully authentic and speak my whole truth. Through whatever form it takes, I recognize that from here on forward, I must relax the terrified grip that I have had around my own throat and lungs, preventing certain words from passing my lips. No longer can I reject the true name of "victim," which follows me as the child who still lives inside my own body. As I stand with my head raised up high in a fuller understanding, I give that inner child the courage to receive the joy and happiness against which she has so often braced herself, believing that if she opened herself fully to life, there would be a price to pay. And I know that as I face my own demons, by the energy of my courage, others will be helped with their horrible secrets, too.

The Power of Secrets Spoken

I stand on a ceremonial bridge speaking to a group of 50 retreat participants. They have already passed over this physical (and symbolic) threshold. Words stick in my throat as I grasp the microphone in my sweaty palm, hearing my voice reverberate eerily through the trees, crackling, like the wind stirring up old, dry leaves. The faces on the other side of this bridge change, some heads dropping visibly with the weight of my words as I speak of being raped at six. Thunder from above our line of vision shakes us further awake. Wakinyan (the thunder beings) urge me onward in this timely stance of alliance. A pesky chipmunk throws little pieces of bark down on me from the tree above, as I cross the mouth of the bridge and tentatively rise along its hoop into the waiting embrace of the others . . . .

Within an hour, one man breaks down in long, seemingly unprovoked sobs. As the entire group holds a supportive container, I sit with him, eyes wide with captivated presence. He honors the movement of tears that come in waves, over and over, until finally, he speaks in a very tiny voice, one finding its expression for the first time. In spite of the horror found in his recollection of childhood abuse, there is also a welcomed relief from the heaviness held beneath his voice for so many years.

Most often, to acknowledge sexual abuse as an adult is easier to bear than to continue carrying the weight of it as the inner child self. For some of us, those disturbing memories remain locked in our inner darkness until we utilize the power of the 5th Key to bring them into conscious light.

Later that week, long after we returned to our homes after the retreat, a woman left a heartfelt message on my voicemail: "Donna, you may not know the impact your words have had . . . more than your words, the fact that I know you and see what a healthy and happy life you lead—that gives me the courage. This is the week that I begin therapy to try to come to terms with the sexual abuse I had within my family. Thank you for sharing what you did." Many more calls, notes, and conversations resulted from those few pivotal moments on the ceremonial bridge. As we know, one pebble dropped in the proverbial pond sends ripples beyond our perceived point of impact.

I first confided to intimate friends and professionals about the ritual nature of my abuse many, many years ago. Remembering this particular Pathways retreat over 20 years ago, I realize that I have even spoken out publically. I just haven't told the whole truth.

Breaking the Vow of Silence

Throughout the process of personal individuation and collective growth, we straddle boundaries between the reality we know and the potential that lies within us. Whether our wounds paralyze us or serve as catalysts for a productive life depends upon our translation of them. We can hold on, white-knuckled, to old paradigms that no longer serve us, or we can open to the fullness of new possibilities. We are not simply at the mercy of what happened to us; our reactions to those occurrences hold power and have their own consequences. Just as I have experienced, the energy for healing is within your grasp. Your greatest wound may certainly contain your greatest gifts. You need only to reach out . . . and gently, lovingly hold your Self.

Healing is sequential and progressive, building in layers. I experienced the antithesis of the experience of losing my voice when I told my mother about the abuse before the first *Pathweavers* retreat over 20 years ago, when I attended a storytelling workshop led by internationally acclaimed master storyteller, Laura Simms.[64] The weekend actively engaged the playful creativity of my inner child with the magic of story, enabling me to open more fully to the emotions that still lay untapped within me. As I awoke on the last day, 12/11/11, the morning after a powerful lunar eclipse, a story bubbled into my consciousness, spilling onto the page almost exactly as it is recorded at the end of this section. There was no contemplation, no pushing it to surface, no great effort. My inner child had found her outside voice!

When Laura encouraged me to read it out loud, I had difficulty speaking my emotionally charged story. She spontaneously asked the other participants to gather around me, and as the small group drew in very, very close, they were able to hear my little voice emerging through the overwhelming emotion, and I could hear the very sound of their breath taking it all in. They willingly sustained the intensity of the moment, helping the stifling emotional dam to break and allowing decades of contained grief to spill forth in deep, uncontainable sobs in between my brutally honest words. When I had read all my pages, I felt completely spent from the power of the sadness and the grief that had, at long last, found their rightful expression.

Laura then invited these eight people to reflect my story back to me. Taking turns as they were moved to, they each shared a piece, retelling word-for-word what I had just said to them. The contrast of male and female voices was indescribably healing; I felt gently held within a close circle of validation and love. In spite of so many years of therapeutic healing work, both as client and as guide, it was in this makeshift container that I was most able to access my deepest pain. It was here that I was able to speak and be heard, held in a remarkably soothing presence. It was the single most powerful piece of my healing facilitated by others, because this clan gave me their all while witnessing a part of my life normally hidden from view.

So, Let Me Tell You a Story

There once was a girl who was young, and fresh, and curious—she loved the adventure of life! When she was about waist high, about six years old, she left the safety of her home and began to explore the world around her. Not long after, while she was still so fresh and new, the little girl was entrusted to people who cared for her during too-long days. But these people were not what they seemed to be.

Unbeknownst to her parents, these people hurt the little girl.

They hurt her in ways which tore her skin,

They hurt her in ways which strained her muscles.

They hurt her in ways which ached her bones.

They hurt her in ways which went deep down

into the teeny, tiny places

within her sweet heart

. . . and that is where the pain lived, sleeping, for a very long time.

But there is another part of the story:

Because when the hurt girl lay crumpled, trembling on hard, cold steps, and feeling very alone,

a candle said, "Come into my flame. Let me warm your chilled bones and soothe your pain."

And when the girl had been pinned by a very heavy weight upon her small body, she

smelled dirt right next to her face, and the dirt said,

"Don't worry, I will hold you up."

And as her young tears fell upon a rock, the rock said, "I feel your pain."

And another time when the girl was being hurt, a magnificent bird, with the softest wings,

came to her and said, "Climb upon my back and hold on. I will take you far, far away to the

gentle mountain who knows how to heal all things."

And together they flew into the distant horizon.

So even though the little girl was very hurt, she never felt completely alone again.

Now, this girl's story is not something that you would yell over to your neighbor

across the fence.

It is not a story that you would tell your friend over tea.

It is not a story you would whisper to your children at bedtime.

The girl's story was unspeakable.

Yet, as the still-curious girl grew,

she traveled far and wide,

and she found a clan who knew the ways of the earth, and the rocks, and even the fire.
They understood the meaning of one's tears.

A very old man with wisdom as long as his beard
gave the girl her true name.
Wakenyape maka wichenope—
Earth Star Rising.
And one day,
*Wakenyape maka wichenope—*Earth Star Rising
felt something rumble in her belly, "grrrr," like a giant force ready to explode.

And one day,
*Wakenyape maka wichenope—*Earth Star Rising
felt something move within her heart,
and the pain that had been sleeping for a very long time,
began to stretch and yawn.

And one day,
Wakenyape maka wichenope
felt something tingle in the place between her heart and her throat—her high heart—
the place where the compassion of one's heart
begins to move into form.

She felt something tingle there,
and then she saw two white birds point their beaks upward,
and move up and through her throat,
until they popped out her mouth
and flew to freedom.

"Your wound has become your strength," a *strong* and *gentle* voice said.

And THAT is how
I came to tell you this story,
today.[65]

5th Key to Wholeness: breaking the silence to share our truth

Undoubtedly we have no questions to ask which are unanswerable.
We must trust the perfection of the creation, so far, as to believe that whatever curiosity
the order of things has awakened in our minds, the order of things can satisfy.
Every man's condition is a solution in hieroglyphic to those inquiries he would put.
He acts it as life, before he apprehends it as truth.

- Ralph Waldo Emerson

If you have experienced trauma that is still unresolved, it is very important that when seeking those with whom you can be honest with regarding your past, you are cautiously selective who you choose, certain that those you divulge your secrets to will hold them with respect in the highest degree. You don't need someone half listening, distracted by thoughts about what they will say next, or those who would be careless with your personal information, spreading it around haphazardly. Caring people can sometimes be clumsy in their support, and that is just fine, but you need someone who will show up *for you*, present to your process. To share your most intimate wounds with one who is immature or cannot be trusted is to open yourself up to being wounded again. In Key #1, you generated a list of support people. Revisit and refine that list now, knowing who you might turn to when you need support or when exploring the transformational aspect of Key #5: breaking the silence to speak your truth.

Be patient and persistent in your self-work and your self-care, as this is one of the greatest projects you could ever embark upon; you are literally revealing the beautiful masterpiece that is your truest Self and allowing your light to shine freely into the world. Edward Edinger encourages us by saying, "Modern man is obliged to proceed in much the same way as the alchemist . . . . The goal is to redeem by conscious realization, the hidden Self . . . ."[66]

I have told my truth . . . breaking the unrighteous pact of silence. The terror that was held for so long is now exposed, and my terrible secret has escaped. Speaking about my early wounding is still very scary, and yet I know as I open the inner dungeons that hold captive the abuse, those dark, dank spaces open to the illumination of the light. After a life-long, fragmented inner storm, there is finally a radiant rainbow appearing with the promise of an integrated tomorrow.

Write Your Own Story

There are many useful ways to write about your own wounds:

- You can choose one incident.
- You can choose a particular time of your life (such as fifth grade, going off to college, or getting your divorce).
- You can focus on a theme or topic and pull info from various times of your life. For example, "the fear of the dark" or "feeling invisible in your lover relationships."
- You can write at a particular time of the day (such as first thing in the morning) and just be with whatever comes up. This morning practice has been sanctioned by many wise teachers as a good way to access what wants to express through you. Julia Cameron's instruction regarding "morning pages"[67] is helpful if you are unfamiliar with this idea.

Don't be concerned about the format:

- You can write in full sentences and paragraphs.
- Or jot lists or phrases that come to you.
- You can even just record single words as they arise.

This is a powerful process:

- Our words are powerful, and if we pause to consider their meaning, they can often point us in a viable and valuable direction. Trust your own process.
- You can use the structure modeled by my storytelling piece and describe your wounding or wounding/healing in a "Once Upon a Time" format. When talking about painful things, sometimes putting yourself in the mindset of telling a story can help you open to the deeper recesses of what exists within you, accessing and

expressing the most difficult content.

- Once your story is recorded, it is important to give yourself some time and space to consider what you want to do with your writing. Sometimes the process of writing is just for you, and the content is not to be shared. At other times, you may want to read it to a close friend or partner or bring it to an appointment and share it with your counselor or coach.

Listening

In the 5th Key to Wholeness, we open the channels to true and wholesome communication, exploring another facet of effective communication—the aspect of listening. We gather information while listening to others, and when we do speak, we hope to be heard in the same vein as what we intend. Truly being heard is a validating experience, and being witnessed in our most painful places is a powerful thing, as demonstrated by my storytelling workshop experience.

- Practice listening and being heard.
- You can do this with a friend or partner in a dialogue where you reflect back what you heard the other person saying, and they respond by clarifying. It is amazing how sometimes what you think you heard is not what the other person said!
- The purpose of this dialogue is not to rush through content, but rather to savor the journey. (As you practice listening to another, you cultivate the ability to listen to all the various parts of you, too!)
- Once you have listened, reflected, and refined what you have heard, then switch roles. You speak, and the other person listens and reflects back to you what you have said, without changing the content of your words.

- This is not about repeating word-for-word what is said, but about capturing the essence of those words.

- On the other hand, when I was supported within the workshop, the others did repeat back my story almost exactly as I had said it. Hearing my own words spoken in various voices with expression conveying understanding was powerfully healing.

- You may wish to try this direct repetititon technique with your partner also, to experience the power of your words.
- Coaches and counselors often offer responses and guidance in terms that are similar to the client's own speech patterns. Hearing familiar, resonate terms can be wonderfully accepting and nurturing.

When someone gets hurt or sustains a trauma, people who know her sometimes don't know what to say or do. If a loved one dies or a tragedy occurs, the "right" thing to say may be quite elusive. Being available to listen can be the kindest gift to offer a friend or loved one. Rather than searching for the right answer or solution to someone else's difficulty, our job is simply to care about her physical suffering or emotional pain. So many wounded ones do not speak, because what happened to them seems unspeakable . . . listening can be pivotal to healing, and effective listening sets the stage for building intimacy, a fertile environment for deeper disclosure.

In the rare instances when I have shared my story with another, I have seen them buckle with the weight of it. In contrast, one relative stranger, a woman I met a couple of years ago at a writing retreat, spoke the most soothing words possible when she supported me by saying that she heard me, she understood what I was saying, and she could not begin to imagine what that experience was like, but that she "would forevermore carry it with her." As she said those gentle words, a huge emotional weight stirred and lifted ever-so-slightly, creating new space. This woman is an exemplar of caring and compassion. She did not have to "do" anything; the sweet nectar of her sincere words gave me nourishment and strength.

I Scream

Isn't it fascinating how our unconscious mind and our buried emotions communicate with us? Their important messages may often be cryptic, and yet when you turn your focus toward them, they can become blatantly clear in their own curious and sometimes comical way! Such was the case when I realized that one of my most favorite things in childhood was ice cream. My grandparents owned a luncheonette with several large tubs always on hand in the front by the take-out window. I could beg for a scoop just about anytime I wanted! So, no surprise that ice cream is still considered one of my comfort foods. One particularly challenging day, while creating a list of the things I wanted to do to support myself, I scribbled the words "I Scream" because I wanted to get my favorite treat. Looking back over the list, I noticed an ironic coincidence: could ice cream be an unconscious code for "I Scream?"

You can use my words to invite a deeper communication with your own inner child, or you can come up with your own words to "play" with. This is how I explored further what so innocently fell onto my sheet of paper asking to be noticed:

- First, I used the words as an acronym, taking each letter and forming a word that related to my wounding.
- I think it is important to move through this kind of exercise quickly, writing whatever pops into your head, rather than taking a long time to think about it. The deepest parts of us communicate in this spontaneous manner. The results can be surprising!

- Here is my list:
  I—Irritability
  S—Sadness
  C—Control
  R—Rage
  E—Endometriosis
  A–Ageless
  M—Migraines

- Then, I went back and wrote words that related to my healing. Here is my list:
  I—Insight
  S—Sensitivity
  C—Compassion
  R—Reality (what is really real?)
  E—Empowerment
  A—Allowing (and trusting)
  M—Many blessings in life!

- You will notice that I embellished my second list in a couple of places. That is OK. Also, you may want to journal after this kind of process, weaving together the information that surfaces.

- For example, I noticed that "ageless" came up in my wounding list. Through my journaling, I surmised that regardless of how old I grow to be, there is still an ageless part of abuse. I need not stay stuck there, but until I deal with the wounded child, she remains. I don't "outgrow" the abuse.

- Repeat this process as many times as you wish. You may bring up more information each time.

Throat Chakra Healing

The extent to which we are able to put our traumatic experiences into words (or images) can be significant and, in some cases, essential to the healing process. Once a word or an image is present with us, we can acknowledge it, hear or see it, and then help it to move forward. Finding the words to describe abuse or acknowledge our pain and suffering can be difficult.

Clear communication is based on a very important principle: say what you mean, and mean what you say! If you practice saying what you *really* mean, and saying it with words that aptly describe what you want to say, in a tone that communicates the feelings behind your words, you will open your Throat Chakra further. An important part of the 5th Key is to stop saying things that you don't really mean, and only say what you do mean.

And when you say something, stand behind your words. If, in the moment, you hear something escape your mouth that is not what you intended, you can clarify or correct it on the spot. Avoid being wishy-washy or putting forth confusing ideas by saying one thing and then, later, the exact opposite. Practice congruency in thought and words, only putting forth messages that you intend. This practice can be much more difficult than it seems!

And if the thought of being "real" or authentic terrifies you, working with a professional trained in trauma therapies can be invaluable.

It is also helpful to observe what words seemingly spill out of your mouth unintentionally that have, upon reflection, personal meaning. Like in our little game with the "I Scream" acronym, the unconscious may try to make itself known, and when you are attentive to it you can discover great insight in just a few little "random" words. Thoughts and beliefs that are hidden from view still continue to affect your behavior; and weaving in those dangly fragments helps you to be more unified and congruent in word and action. Accessing what has been held within, abandoned, or rejected, and turning attention there can have lasting results—impacting how you feel about yourself, the kind of work you do, how successful you are, the health of your relationships, and ultimately, your happiness level. Open to receive more of the goodness and the bounty of life as you learn ways to express your fullest authenticity.

In this 5th energy center, the Throat Chakra, we can gather power for speaking our personal truth and for finding the healing inherent in letting go of any long-held, destructive secrets. Yet, as you talk about your personal story and your particular pain or suffering, be careful not to become self-absorbed in your pain or stuck in your story of wounding. We have a responsibility not only to ourselves, but also to the collective, to find the meaning in our experiences and then to sculpt them into something useful— a building block for our greater success and happiness. As we bond together in the light of our personal truths, we can create cultural shifts that uplift the quality of our human condition.

Your truth matters.

Breathe slowly, in and out, for three or four breath cycles. Imagine the red ray of the first power center grounding you into the earth beneath you. Imagine the orange ray of the second power center also moving downward as it invigorates your creative ability to manifest a healthy life. Imagine the yellow ray rising within your third center as it radiates out through all parts of you, bringing meaning and purpose to your life. Imagine the green hue of your heart essence flowing easily and gracefully from your heart center through all the parts of you and beyond, reaching out to touch others. Now imagine that heart essence seasoning your thoughts and words, as the blue radiance of the throat chakra opens to allow clear and healthy communication to be expressed through all you say and do. Speak the following affirmative blessing with gratitude and assurance:

Communication is a precious gift that enables me to share my thoughts, my needs, and my desires. I tap into my most authentic Self and share from the clarity of that unique essence—I speak my honest truth. I am heard in the integrity of my words, and I also honor others by being present and listening intently to what they say to me. My communication is clear and meaningful as I discover and claim my True Voice.

6th Key

Reclaiming the
Sacred Altar

In every crisis, a woman is tempted to become the victim

instead of staying the heroine.

~ Jean Shinoda Bolen[68]

Faith is not about certainty but about courage.

~ Catherine Keller[69]

Through the *Ajna*, Brow, or 3rd Eye Chakra, I am able to see beyond the limitations of my human eyes. Utilizing the 3rd Eye of the brow center and seeing from that deep inner perspective, as well as listening with my inner ear, I am guided to greater understanding. I am able to move past the limited reality of my wounding and its effects. As I look up and into the indigo hue of the 3rd Eye Chakra, I give thanks for intuitive and spiritual truths helping to guide my life's path. I recognize that my spirituality is not limited by location or doctrine, but is truly an integral part of me.

In the realm of the 6th Chakra, the brow chakra, we discover our 6th Key to Wholeness. It is here that we connect with all that is spiritual beyond the confines of a church building or humanity's doctrines. Through the 3rd Eye of the brow we can "see" beyond the physical limitationsto the truth of our being. We can affirm that we carry our own sanctuary within us, tapping into Universal Truths and claiming them as our own. This is not to say that we necessarily reject organized religion or going to church, only that we recognize that our deepest faith is experienced through the personal relationship between each of us, individually, and our Spiritual Source or Divine Essence.

I ask that you pause before you continue reading and begin by touching in with the center of your own beliefs and the truth of your own experience—it is from that centered space that I would like to proceed. Review your ideas about religion and your ideas about spirituality, which may or may not be exactly the same. In what ways are they similar, and in what ways are they different? Then, focus on your religious experience up until this point, reviewing your thoughts and feelings about your personal history. You can take as much time as you need to consider these important questions, and if you'd like, take some time to journal about it.

Inner Guidance / Inner Strength

Our Spiritual Source is literally watching over us. That Divine Intelligence, Wisdom, and Spiritual Truth may take many forms, appearing differently to different people, but it is Universal in nature and belongs to us all. This Divine Source is not separate and external, but rather is connected to and expresses through us.

Even when bad things happen, there is goodness still present, and if we can open our awareness, it will make itself known to us. An elderly Indian, a friend of Gandhi's, told psychologist Carl Jung that some people do not have an outer guru, but rather have "a spirit for a teacher."[70] I learned at a young age to listen to the direction given by my inner spiritual guides, as it was a matter of sheer survival for me to obey their direction.

Because I learned to converse with my guides early on, that relationship has been a natural and easy part of my being, an ability that I do not question. They did not make demands on me, instead offering free will and choice, so I learned to trust this inner guidance, utilizing it in times of crisis and success. Rather than creating dependency, theirs was the very best teaching instruction, helping to build my inner strength and character.

As a psychic athlete, I was trained to successfully make my way in the world, stretching in my capacity to walk on a path of personal integrity, as I answered to the Higher Source within me. I learned to rebel against the status quo, trust my own inner compass, and envision beyond the constraints of what was put before me. With intuition and spiritual awareness developed out of necessity, I grew accustomed to drawing from the strength that speaks to me, *through me*—that which I refer to as my guides or the Guardian Council of Light. This loud and clear, ever-available Inner Source has led me toward multi-dimensional healing and the ability to accept true transformation.

A Child's Innocence is Sacrificed

The terrifying trauma I experienced as a Catholic girl was not just about sexual abuse—the ritualistic nature of it threatened to steal something far more important. In a cruel act by a priest, a Messenger of God, not only was my child-innocence pierced and shattered, but the sacred altar was stolen from me. What was intended as the religious heart of healing and renewal, the now-desecrated altar, became a symbol of dominance, control, and twisted religious rites.

Perverted rituals of pedophile priests sacrifice the very sanctity of our faith, changing it forever. In *Sacrilege*, Leon Podles, a former federal investigator and Christian scholar, talks about New England as having "scores of priest-malefactors, some of whose behavior bordered on madness." Specifically in regards to a "charismatic young priest" at St. Cecilia's Church in Stamford, Connecticut, Podles says that the Rev. Lawrence F.X. Brett liked the combination of sacraments and sex. He lighted candles and said prayers, wrapping his act in the symbols and rituals of the Church.

Continuing, Podles says that "Priests invoked God while abusing children."

> Father Nicholas V. Cudemo of Philadelphia gang raped another victim, and then put the consecrated Host, which Catholics believe to be the very body of Christ, into her vagina, telling her she had "fucked God" or "fucked Jesus," after which he heard her confession.[71]

Thus rigidly polarized good and evil is warped into something very disturbed, yet foundationally grounded in the power of the church and its masculine hierarchy. In this same vein, it seemed that I was offered as a human sacrifice on the Catholic altar. One must ask—a sacrifice for who or what? Was it a twisted act meant for a similarly twisted idea of God? Leon Podles reports about one victim whose psychologist, Joseph F. Roe, could not explain her behavior on a purely psychological basis, instead seeking guidance from her bishop as to "someone who wuld be qualified to discern whether or not she [was] possessed." I wonder about this in light of threats to "take my soul." Father Doyle, Sipe, and Wall speak about the historical evolution of *sacrifice* as a means to requisition the favor of the gods. They report that the spiritual abuse by a priest is often described by victims as a "spiritual devastation," citing Dr. Leslie Lothstein and Leonard Shengold for defining it as "soul murder."[72]

Forgiving God

Engaging in perverted acts "in the name of Jesus Christ," or in some other way connecting the abuse with the Higher Source, places a psychological and spiritual barrier between the victim and God. Religious trappings including statues of saints, stained-glass windows, and an ornate altar with beautiful, sacred objects indicate an intimacy with God, leading us to believe that when we are hurt in such a surrounding, God is at fault. Victims may have an aversion to any organized religion or worse, experience a lifetime of struggling with their own inner faith—because after all, how could God abandon them in His own place of worship?

One would think that faith ripped from a young soul would be forever compromised, yet if we can open our hearts to the essential truth that the abusers had no right to connect Him with their repulsive, sacrilegious acts, we can find our way to forgiving God. Otherwise, the poison of our misdirected bitterness forms a barrier between our Divine Source and us. Furthermore, anger at God—as well as any guilt or shame associated with thinking that we, ourselves, could be at fault for the abuse—has the capacity to rot us from the inside out. This is why it is so important to forgive God, who is as close as your own heart and eternally connected with your own soul. Open to the ways in which He (or She) can show up in support of your life. Your spirituality is an essential part of your nature, and when you reject it, you sadly perpetuate the great harm that was done to you.

I am so very grateful to have found New Thought spirituality so many years ago. The *Science of Mind and Spirit* teachings of Ernest Holmes[73] have allowed me to embrace my childhood wounds and to find the spiritual salve to heal them. I was able to step into a positive role within my church community, as part of the "healing arm" of my church. People, quite literally, pay me to pray, as well as to support them through crisis and to help them create greater states of well-being by re-patterning unhealthy behaviors, healing wounds, meeting life challenges, and better expressing their unique beauty. Having reached the level of licensed Practitioner Emeritus with over 20 years of service, I realize that this church experience has given me a strong base for healing my own wounds, too.

In my chosen church community, destructive ideas of an all-powerful clergy who could do whatever they liked *to you* were replaced by a theology that taught co-creation and, ultimately, personal responsibility. I thrived within this fertile system, which encouraged me to trust and celebrate the wisdom that came to me through my own innate knowing. By the grace of this spiritual discipline, which respects the teachings of all sacred paths, I was able to honor Universal Truths that know no denominational boundaries, and to develop my own personal understanding of God, which remains an integral and central part of my life. Psychologist Marion Woodman says,

> If we dare to ask the question "Who am I?" then we commit ourselves to the

responsibility of honing our way to our own inner truth . . . in the silence of the chrysalis our silver chalice is wrought, the silver chalice that bears the golden child. Pondering in the heart is not a sentimental journey to the Goddess. Pondering in the heart involves the joy and the agony of consciously allowing our own I am to magnify the great I AM.[74]

Open to the change that can come to you as you let go of any sense of the all-powerful Church having a monopoly on God and instead, recognize that within you is the capacity to have your own, very personal, relationship with the Divine.

Reclaiming the Altar

The clear and resonant sound of the crystal heart bowl sings through the quaint and beautiful old church.[75] Soft light dances through shadows, illuminating all with a warm glow, as we bring our spiritual sharing to a close. I am up on the platform of the altar, playing the singing bowl for the culmination of our spiritual celebration with the ministers and over a hundred practitioners, who are gathered for our annual retreat. As the members of our community begin to file out, I once again take a seat in the front right-hand pew. Gazing at the simple, yet elegant altar, I am struck by its sweet beauty.

Bill Loving sits to my right, savoring the warmth of this holy place, and a few minutes later, we are joined by Liz Brower, who sits on my left. With great purpose, my inner guides speak:

"Go to the altar," they say.

At the very moment that I rise to move forward, without any prompting, lovely voices waft from the choir loft above. Carrie MaKenna and Mary Jo Honiotes spontaneously sing sacred songs that are dear to me. These two women are sisters of the soul, and together we have co-facilitated a women's group for almost seven years. My eyes grow wet with the sound of their loving voices. I kneel at the altar and say a silent prayer, speaking as I often do of my love and dedication to Spirit and to my life as a spiritual path.

"It's time," prompts the voice. "It is time to reclaim your altar."

I rise from my knees and step up onto the main platform, bowing with respect, kneeling, and kissing the ground before me. The choir of sister-women shifts gracefully, singing my favorite melody by Ricki Byers-Beckwith,

"Use me, oh God, I stand for you, and here I'll abide as you show me, all that I must do."

I remain with my forehead touching the altar until the song is complete. Then, rising once again, I return to my seat. With Liz on my left (the place of the feminine) and Bill on my right (the place of the masculine), I feel a powerful energy as I am symbolically supported by both. Tears gently stream down my face, washing away the ancient sins of others, perpetrated upon me and left behind as a burden in my care.

Liz is the first to leave, and by the time Bill and I stand to go, we are the only ones left in this quiet chapel. Bill and his wife, Sue, are two of only a handful of people who know what happened to me as a child. As we walk up the gravel drive that leads from the sweet chapel to the retreat lodge where we are spending the night, Bill and I easily share our latest news. Suddenly, Bill stops and faces me on the road with eyes wide with wonderment.

"Donna, you don't know, DO YOU?"

"Know what?" I ask.

"The last group here at St. Malo's—they left just minutes before we arrived— the last group in that chapel—well, they were a group of sexual-offender priests. They were here last week for psychological and spiritual rehabilitation."

Unbelievable!

We marvel at the synchronicity and perfection of a ceremony with no conscious planning, yet obviously so divinely guided that it could use the mix of energies gathered in this Catholic chapel, so I might boldly declare, once and for all, that the sacred altar was now mine.

Miracle Blessings

Years later, in the sanctuary of a little Catholic Church, I knelt at the feet of Mother Mary and prayed. There, at the chapel in Chimayo, New Mexico, I received a bona fide miracle, demonstrating not only that my brother would heal from emergency brain surgery, but that my steps were blessed by Her—my path made clear and open.

On the way home from seeing my Native American teacher, Rob and I decide to stop at a little chapel we heard about in Chimayo. My brother is having surgery today, and I want to offer a prayer in this Catholic sanctuary that I have heard so much about but never visited.

When we pull into the parking lot, we find it empty. After looking around the sparse outer yard for a few minutes and seeing that the area is completely deserted, we stroll naturally through the front gate and enter the church building through the main doorway. I stop to look at the candles flickering with lit intention in the back of the church. Having been raised Catholic, my inclination is to light one for my brother, but they are already aglow with other people's whispered prayers.

I wander to the front and sit in the first row, gazing upon the beautiful main altar. Rob notices a hallway to the left, and we peek down the narrow opening to find a tiny room with a small pit of dirt—a sign on the wall says the dirt is considered sacred. A lone baby food jar sits on the edge of the pit, beckoning me to fill it, and so I do, gently scraping the soft brown granules into the small container. The rich smell of fertile soil tickles my nose.

We explore another hallway containing photos and letters of people who claim to have been healed by the dirt, now cradled inside the baby food container in my pocket. There is even a walker hanging from one of the walls. Lots of canes and braces are strewn about, too, evidence of handicapped limbs that now move freely. We spend a long time in this hall, lingering with the tangible healing energy present here; you can literally feel its potent and magnetic pulse. Funny, but the thought never crosses my mind to pray, because it seems as if this place goes beyond any need for spoken prayer. The profound sanctity of it is beyond words.

As we walk back through the main church, I'm drawn to the left of the main altar to a smaller area set as a mini-altar honoring Mother Mary. I kneel before her and pray for protection and healing for my brother, now in surgery thousands of miles away. As I rise and begin to step away, I come back down onto my knees, "Forgive me, I mean no disrespect. But I have not prayed in exactly this particular way in a long time. Will you please show me a sign to let me know you've heard me?"

As Rob and I exit the inner sanctuary, leaving the church through a hallway vestibule, a door we had not noticed on our left suddenly opens.

"What are you DOING in here?" a small man asks, rather forcibly!

He seems puzzled by our presence, and his voice and demeanor are quite reprimanding, as if we must be up to some mischief. In reaction to our innocent looks, he claims to have locked the door to the church and the gate himself over an hour ago.

I quickly relay the story about my brother having emergency brain surgery, hoping it will at least give us a legitimate reason for being here. As he listens to me, the man inexplicably jerks his head up and to the left, as if looking at something. He then tells us to wait and scurries off, disappearing out of view. When he returns just a moment later, he is carrying an unlit candle. He offers it to me, and I ask if I should place it in the back with the other candles. He immediately agrees, but then jerks his head around, once again up and to the left, pausing as if to listen to an instruction. Then, he says,

"No, put it up front . . . by Mary."

As I walk to the front to place my prayer in the familiar warmth of the candle's glow, tears begin to well up in my eyes and slowly make moist trails down my cheeks. As I place my lit candle at her side, I quietly note that there are no other candles by Mary. Mine is the only glowing light flickering upon her face.

El Santuario, the little chapel we visited, has been called the "Lourdes of America."[76] Now that I've been back to Chimayo several times since, I realize that worshippers and tourists alike cram into every possible space in the small church while it is open. The parking lot is overwhelmed with the clamor of local vendors selling their wares and cars coming and going. The fact that we entered an empty lot that day and were welcomed through both the supposedly-locked front gate and locked front door is really a part of what I consider a small miracle with the Blessed Mother at El Sanctuario. My brother, by the way, gratefully had a swift physical recovery.

One does not have to be a practicing Catholic to appreciate the beautiful energy of healing and the collective sense of faith that is held in these powerfully sacred places. An unexpected result of my impromptu ritual to reclaim the altar at St. Malo has been that I am now able to find solace in visiting different Catholic sanctuaries. I grew to understand that my anger at the Catholic Church, although justified in a sense, also unfairly judged the Church as a whole. Any church is made up of many people, and each person within the church is responsible for his or her own behavior. Many religious men and women have done valuable work from within the container of this organization—Mother Theresa is a fine example. As I came to terms with my own healing, I found welcoming in these sacred spots, which possessed positively charged spiritual energy. The Day of the Dead celebration in Mexico, a remarkable Taizé ceremony at the Chapel of the Holy Cross in Sedona, Arizona, and Mother Cabrini Shrine in Golden, Colorado have all had a profound spiritual impact on me.

The 3rd Eye for Healing

One transformational quality found in the 6th Key to Wholeness is the power of self-reflection. Using the intuition and in-sight of the 3rd Eye, we can identify and consider our truest beliefs and deeply personal feelings about spirituality. We examine how we think and feel about the value of established teachings and doctrine, as well as the power of individuals to access truth from within themselves through their own spiritual connection. We consider if the need to suffer is a God-given requirement to build character and prove our faith and if the act of suffering, itself, serves some higher purpose in cleansing our "sins." And we can explore what constitutes a "sin" and whether we believe in the concept of sin, or whether we view our mistakes and transgressions in another light. We can contrast these ideas about suffering with the notion of the joy of living producing useful energy. And how could our happiness and joy serve our Spiritual Source (God, Buddha, Creator, Great Mystery . . .)? In the illumination of the 3rd Eye, we can even consider the idea of power and domination versus the idea of appropriate em-power-ment of an individual. What are *your* thoughts on those topics?

Whether or not it occurred in a religious setting, your wounding may ultimately serve as a productive "sacrifice" of an old way, in order to birth a newer way of being. Unfortunately, too many of us become stuck in the grief or horror of what happened to us. In a misguided attempt to justify our pain as necessary suffering for our spiritual good, we may even perpetuate it. On the other end of the spectrum, we may also perpetuate our own suffering when we try to avoid feeling the pain altogether. When we stop running and stand our ground, looking at the face of our wound, inspecting its features for obvious and hidden lessons and feeling the emotions we find there, then true healing can occur.

Gather the lists that you have created. If they are in one notebook or journal, this will be easy!

- Look at the list of the people you can draw in for support.
- Review the list of your physical symptoms, your wounding, and the emotions you

observe when you lash out or express with a vengeance. Now is the time to ponder how you might actively move through the stages of re-patterning these behaviors and life experiences.

- You may be able to accomplish these shifts on your own, with conscious and purposeful choice. Or you may need help from a trained professional.

- Explore your ideas of the meaning of the words "church," "sanctuary," and "altar." If the source of your wounding happened in a church, explore how that wounding shaped your feelings about religion.

- Explore what "spirituality" means to you separate from a church building or an organized community.

- Note your spiritual practices. These may be different for each of us. Some people I know find a spiritual connection through playing their music or having their hands in the dark soil of the earth. Tap into that inner place within you that recognizes your spirituality, even if it comes in an unusual form.

- Our process of clearing and evolving is not easy, but it is well worth it. There is so much more to life . . . so much more to you. Keep moving, allowing your evolution its path!

- And please know that I support you in this valuable endeavor and am cheering you on. I trust that Spirit is working in and through your life.

- No one had the right to take the sanctity of the altar from you. In your own time, in your own way, claim the sacred altar within you, and be open to an outer community who can honor that part of you as it celebrates your spiritual nature.

- Not all church communities see through a constrictive lens. Be open to the exact right church or community group to join you in celebration and spiritual practice.

Those Seeking Change

The Catholic Church, historically, has been a strong example of patriarchal dominance, at times demonstrating an outright dismissal of the significance of women and children. Blinded by the ego-lens of power and dominance, the Church lost its way, failing to remember to ask, "Who do we serve?" Abuse of the innocents is forcing us to cross the previously protected sanctity of the church's boundaries and ask this and other difficult questions, individually and collectively.

We have seen much upheaval within the Catholic Church as it lashes back at those attempting to shift the status quo and bring forth positive change from within its ranks. Jungian scholar and women's advocate, Jean Shinoda Bolen, speaks of a present-day inquisition by the church. She says that during the original inquisition, "the first to be burned at the stake were the wise women, midwife-healers." She speaks about the "officially sanctioned torture" lasting for five and a half centuries. Bolen cites Matthew Fox when saying,

> The same office that conducted the Inquisition (the Congregation for the Doctrine of Faith) is conducting an investigation of North American nuns. The Vatican announced in 2009 that there would be an apostolic visitation to investigate the religious life and beliefs of communities affiliated with the Leadership Conference of Women's Religious (LCWR), representing about 95 percent of the 68,000 nuns in North America.

Bolen continues saying,

> This investigation was preceded by the denunciation of Reiki, Therapeutic Touch, Healing Touch and Centering Prayer, which are among practices used by many Catholic nursing sisters and retreat centers affiliated with the Leadership Conference [and] that such practices could be "of Satan" is a scary medieval accusation.[77]

Much like the midwives being accused of wrongdoing because they tried to relieve what was believed to be divinely ordained suffering in childbirth, the Church's position seems little more than a misguided lashing out to discredit good work. The only "sin" the sisters commit with these practices is that they often empower the individual (patient), as opposed to cultivating his or her dependence on the power of the Catholic Church. The comfort accomplished through these well-established healing modalities serves many people in times of pain and hardship. Once again, we have a modern-day witch hunt.

On April 18, 2012, the Congregation for the Doctrine of the Faith completed their four-year assessment of the Leadership Conference of Women Religious (LCWR), revealing that they found "serious doctrinal problems" and the need for reform. Adding to this transitional mix was a midstream shift in papal leadership, with the potential for a new perspective, but those in power continue to speak publically of a desire to squelch what they call "radical feminism" in the form of programs and presentations sponsored by the LCWR.

Sister Pat Farrell, the past president of the LCWR spoke with Bob Simon for a 60 Minutes report broadcasted on Sunday, March 17, 2013. Sister Pat shared that American nuns want to be given more important responsibilities in their parishes and in the other institutions they serve, an idea that bucks the long-standing interpretation of Church law, so the interviewer asked the nun whether her desire compromised the vow of obedience she took when she entered religious life. "Well, I think this is one of the areas of misunderstanding and difference. Our first obedience is to God," she tells Simon. "What we obey is God and God's call to us as expressed in so many different sources—it's not just the teaching authority of the Church, although that is certainly a legitimate part of it." Sister Pat believes that something else may be motivating the men in the Vatican: "I don't know, but it feels to me like fear. What would happen if women really were given a place of equality in the Church?"[78]

In another news interview, the controversial Sister Simone Campbell, noted educator and Executive Director of NETWORK, repeatedly used the phrase "God's green earth,"[79] which directly relates to the Feminine Essence introduced in Key #1. In contrast to the cooperative ways of the natural world, patriarchal business and government sometimes focus on the needs and desires of a few rather than the good of the whole, resulting in rampant devastation of our natural resources, which puts our entire planet in jeopardy. The Catholic Church is just one hierarchical system that demonstrates an egocentric, self-serving approach. You can help tip the scale back toward balance by letting go of any sense of the all-powerful Church having a monopoly on God and rather recognizing that within you is the capacity to have your own, very personal relationship with the Divine.

Returning to the Sacred Garden

Ethnopsychologist Joanna Macy speaks about *The Great Turning*, which she describes as "the essential adventure of our time: the shift from the industrial growth society to a life-sustaining civilization." Macy speaks about the need to feel our personal and collective pain with regard to the devastation of our earth, so we can turn to the process of healing the planet. When we are not overburdened by our own unresolved pain, we can open our hearts to the grieving of the earth and face the consequences of what humanity has done to her. When we temper human arrogance and re-pattern our collective behavior, we can better plan for a sustainable future.[80]

My Native teachers see themselves reflected in the world around them, recognizing that there is no separation between the individual soul and the *anima mundi*, the soul of the world. Modern man has an urgent need to re-establish this essential connection, seeing life as an inescapable, organic whole. Depth Psychologist Dr. Stephen Aizenstat reports a disturbing fact—that 18 year olds tested can identify up to 500 corporate logo images and less than 12 indigenous species commonly found in their own backyard. Aizenstat claims the corporate logos possess a "terminator gene," because their primary purpose is to sell something; basically, these logos are empty images except for their marketing potential. A renowned expert on images, Aizenstat says that our rich and vibrant connection to the earth is vitally alive and something that offers us great value; yet, this ancient relationship between people and the natural world, in many cases, is being virtually bought off and lost in our modern time.[81]

You can help by:

- Developing your own relationship with the natural world all around you.
- Observing the colors, sounds, smells, and textures of the plants, trees, and flowers.

- Noticing how birds and animals behave and how they interact with each other. One day, I watched with fascination when the little squirrel in my cottonwood tree defended his turf from an entire flock of crows. As the larger birds hovered over him, I marveled at his boldness as he continued to chatter, chasing them off the limb. After a bit, they tired of the game and flew away.
- Remembering that everything in nature has meaning, and that each piece is important to the whole. Observing the natural flow of life can tell us a lot about our own character!

- One process I like to use with groups is to gather in a circle and proclaim our awareness of and appreciation for a particular part of nature. We do this by saying, "I speak my word for _____." I speak my word for the rain. I speak my word for the mountain. Or, I speak my word for dolphins. As we mention these aspects by name, we honor them, reminding ourselves of their importance in the overall scheme.
- You can create a collage with pictures from magazines showing some of your favorite things in the natural world. Isn't it interesting that so many of us are drawn to uniquely different and unusual species, such as the red-legged tree frogs or the amazingly-cute baby hedgehogs? Perhaps through appreciating their differences, we are able to embrace our own.

- We are each called as Earth Guardians, stewards of her various expressions, taking care of them for the future.
- Back up your personal exploration of the natural world by supporting individuals and organizations that work for conservation and sustainability for our future.
- Every day, in many ways, walk with respect and appreciation on the ground beneath you, connecting with all that is around you, and giving thanks for the beauty and the richness of our natural world.
- As you support her, she will synergistically support you with encouraging signs from the natural world and the healing capacity of the very earth beneath your feet (described in detail in Key #1).

6th Key to Wholeness: reclaiming the sacred altar

Religion is a belief in someone else's experience;

spirituality is having your own experience.

~ Deepak Chopra[82]

Truth is found in the very spark of life that crosses all man-made boundaries to the very essence expressed in all its many different forms. Life abounds with spiritual opportunity for deepening our understanding and our faith—this is the Path of the Sacred. There is no one direction you must traverse and no one destination you must reach. Rather, it is a journey you can embark upon right here and right now; it begins wherever you are, in the moment you embrace its potential, and life itself carries you onward! When we have no idea which way to go or how to find what we need, if we just believe in the possibility, our way will be made known to us.

When you are totally overwhelmed, look to the outer signs in "God's green earth"—the natural world around you— and you may be inspired by the wind moving gently through a mighty oak or the luminous shimmering of dragonflies' wings. Open to finding resolution and healing, and the Infinite Source, which no knows limits and is not bound by the illusive walls of any church, will show you the righteous way. Hold the vision for your life having a spiritual pattern, and marvel at the way your sacred path unfolds. Alter your idea of the altar as being in a specific location in a man-made building, and instead recognize that the sacred altar lives, forevermore, within your heart of hearts and your deepest soul. Your blessed ceremony of celebration is found in the very breath you breathe, and in each step you take; your life is the expression of your sacred connection with God. How can you bring forth your most authentic God-given expression?

Right now, in this moment, take the time to breathe slowly and consciously, in and out, for three or four breath cycles. Imagine the red ray of the first power center grounding you with the sacred earth beneath you, and imagine the orange ray of the second power center as it invigorates your creative ability to manifest a healthy life. Imagine the yellow ray of your third center offering meaning and purpose and the green heart essence seasoning everything you say and do. Visualize the blue of the throat center bringing clarity of expression through the power of your words as you express your most authentic self. Now, imagine the deep indigo of the 3rd Eye Chakra shining forth from your forehead, like a guiding light, showing you the rightful path. Speak the following affirmative blessing with gratitude and assurance:

I am able to see beyond the limitations of my human eyes, utilizing the 3rd Eye of the brow. And also I listen with the wisdom of my inner ear. I am guided to move beyond worldly constraints, seeking a greater reality. The purpose of my healing is to reveal the strong and resilient core within me, and so I accept all that has happened to me as a significant part of my growth; each piece is only one part of who I am as a whole, vibrant person. I know and accept that I carry my altar within me always, and that I can access it through my very breath, and my every step, in any given moment. As I look up and into the indigo hue of the 3rd Eye Chakra, I give thanks for the intuitive and spiritual truths that guide my life's path.

7ᵗʰ Key
Recognizing and Living from Oneness

A new tribe of people shall come unto the earth from many colors, classes, creeds,
who by their actions and deeds, shall make the earth green again.
They will be known as the Warriors of the Rainbow.

~ Hopi Prophecy

Remember to look up—there may be a rainbow waiting for you!

~ Donna DeNomme

In the connected energy of the *Sahasrara* or Crown Chakra, I tap awakened psychic awareness of the unity between my human form and the higher essence of All-of-Creation. My search for meaning and true purpose is realized as I come to know more of who I am and who I can be. I sense understanding, beyond my limited personal scope, as I recognize that I am a conduit for receiving heavenly inspiration and divine energies here on earth. I realize that every person I meet and every event I experience is significant to the greater plan; therefore, I choose my actions wisely, attempting to balance my human condition with innate spiritual wisdom, acting from a state of grace. I move beyond personal limitations as I look at my past and present, analyzing its content, assimilating the greater potential of its occurrence, and opening to the new growth it catalyzes. I accept that I am an intergral part of the Divine Plan.

We have explored the valuable multi-dimensional perspective of the human chakra system, moving back and forth between the microcosm of personal experience and its macrocosmic potential. We have seen through the eyes of the healer, finding meaning in each and every step. All along, we have recognized a core message that says,

> **"Don't get stuck in the story of wounding . . . .**
> **The point is found in the healing of that wound."**

In the Crown Chakra, located at the very top of the head, we discover the 7th Key to Wholeness: our Oneness with all of life. Do you have an innate sense of connection with what is around you? Or do you see your life as solo, having no particular impact on the outer world? The understanding of the 7th Key unlocks a perspective that travels beyond our solitary personal scope and the reality of our limited human condition, and accesses our true and infinite life potential. Let's follow the golden thread that stretches above the top of our heads into the heavens. Recognize that those lofty possibilities begin right here and right now within the solid density of our human existence. We can learn much about the vastness of that potential by beginning with what appear to be opposites.

The Intersection of Opposites

There is often more than one perspective in a story, and there is usually more than one perspective in life, too. Yet people often look at the world through a stark lens of comparisons and contrast: bad and good, guilty and innocent, adult and child, perpetrator and victim, or aggressor and wounded. These perspectives limit our understanding, compartmentalizing people into labeled categories, while missing the broad range of what is possible within each of us.

Even when we are considered "good," we each still possess the capacity to cause harm; the possibility for what we see in others is a part of our human condition as well. What we abhor in him, her, or them lives at least as a potential reality within ourselves. The fact that it disgusts or revolts us may be because there is a tiny speck of that same quality within us, even though we think we reject it altogether. What we despise may even be an unexpressed inclination that we have buried very, very deep inside, cringing at the very thought that any part of that might be who we are.

Perhaps we even leaned toward that inclination at another time, in another place, and have brought that distant memory in, desperately trying to prevent it from happening again! Beloved philosopher Lao-Tzu says it beautifully:

> He who feels punctured
> Must once have been a bubble,
> He who feels unarmed
> Must have carried arms,
> He who feels belittled
> Must have been consequential
> He who feels deprived
> Must have had privilege . . . .[83]

When we open to the value found in what appears to be dark and twisted, painful or wounding, then we can also recognize that without those who disappointed us, abandoned, betrayed, or abused us, we would not have been able to evolve in the same way. This perspective does not necessarily forgive what has happened; it just provides us with a broader view of the purpose and value of our wounding (Key #3). When we consider the interface of what appears to be opposite but is still relative, we can develop a more useful understanding.

Although people hurt themselves all the time, it takes a greater sense of betrayal or wounding, penetrating from the outside in, to leave us with a feeling of repulsion or separation from the "other." It takes an external sword piercing us to our very core to enable us to access the depths of the universal wound of separation. When this occurs, we find ourselves alone in a barren and solitary desert, searching for fluid drops of life-sustaining hope, so that we may evolve full circle by rediscovering the essential truth of our luscious and vital interconnection with all of life. This is the human dilemma, and each of us, in our own way, makes the difficult journey with its great potential for healing. Although some of us are given a more difficult or complex experience, we each encounter the task!

At times, it may even be by pushing against the challenge (or in our resistance to it) that we realize our truest potential. We might choose a direction that would otherwise not be pursued, as is often seen when people study healing modalities because of their own pain. We explored this idea in describing the motivation of the Wounded Healer in Key #3, and we realized that through adversity, unconscious interests or abilities can be forced by necessity to the surface and become more fully developed. The difficulty of life is not simply tragic when we examine it from the perspective that if we are here to learn and grow, even our most traumatic experiences are significant to our overall progress. And if even our most traumatic experiences are important, then those who hurt or take advantage of us play a necessary role.

We consider basic archetypal patterns that repeat over and over throughout time. Abandonment, betrayal, and abuse are traumas that, in some way, touch each of us. Regardless of which side of the equation we are on at any given time, we are learning about and working through the patterns of these universal blueprints. Our task is to bring forth greater understanding to shift and heal these repetitive archetypal patterns, furthering the expression of their evolution. We look at the symbolic value of all parts of life, seeing the value of each person in every story. The Buddhist monk, Thich Nhat Hanh, says it poignantly when presenting his awakened concept of life in *Please Call Me by My True Names*:

> Don't say that I will depart tomorrow—
> even today I am still arriving.

> Look deeply: every second I am arriving
> to be a bud on a Spring branch,
> to be a tiny bird, with still-fragile wings,
> learning to sing in my new nest,
> to be a caterpillar in the heart of a flower,
> to be a jewel hiding itself in a stone.

> I still arrive, in order to laugh and to cry,
> to fear and to hope.
> The rhythm of my heart is the birth and death
> of all that is alive.

I am a mayfly metamorphosing
on the surface of the river.
And I am the bird
that swoops down to swallow the mayfly.

I am a frog swimming happily
in the clear water of a pond.
And I am the grass-snake
that silently feeds itself on the frog.

I am the child in Uganda, all skin and bones,
my legs as thin as bamboo sticks.
And I am the arms merchant,
selling deadly weapons to Uganda.

I am the twelve-year-old girl,
refugee on a small boat,
who throws herself into the ocean
after being raped by a sea pirate.
And I am the pirate,
my heart not yet capable
of seeing and loving.

I am a member of the politburo,
with plenty of power in my hands.
And I am the man who has to pay
his "debt of blood" to my people
dying slowly in a forced labor camp.

My joy is like Spring, so warm
it makes flowers bloom all over the Earth.
My pain is like a river of tears,
so vast it fills the four oceans.

Please call me by my true names,
so I can hear all my cries and laughter at once,

so I can see that my joy and pain are one.

Please call me by my true names,

so I can wake up,

and the door of my heart

could be left open,

the door of compassion.[84]

The fact is that when we see ourselves as separate, it is much easier to hold bitterness and resentment for those who harmed us. Indeed, this perspective is the prevailing idea in many places around the world; an approach that keeps us locked in a cycle of wounding and re-wounding in a misguided attempt to make it all "right." But this stance also holds us captive in being the victim, preventing us from fully healing. It is forever "us" and "them."

The honest truth is that we each, in our own way, are wounded, and perhaps also wound others. Even the very best of us who attempt to live with kindness may still wound others. In a moment of anger, is there a mild form of abuse? Is there ever a time when we take advantage of another? The more aware we are of our own behavior, the more able we are to tip the balance in the direction we choose.

One remarkable aspect of compassion that we might discover while pausing at the intersection of the opposites is the healing capacity of empathy. Empathy is the ability to infer how something might be seen or felt from another person's perspective, as if we are able to be with their experience from a point of exceptional observation, virtually seeing the situation through their eyes. This doesn't mean we agree with or condone their behavior, but instead are open to how those choices and actions might have happened and what significance it has from their perspective. By moving past our own resistance and any need to be the injured party, we dive head on into the terrifying darkness of a vast and deep pool. Not surprisingly, it is often here that we might discover information that could help us prevent the reoccurrence of such horrific behavior in the future. With the freedom found through compassion and empathy, we move past the rigidity of painful and limiting wounds into the freshness of healing discovery.

When we can empathize with even our worst "enemies," we can journey from the intellect to compassion, beyond the logic of our minds to the understanding of our hearts. This journey is an integral one, one that is essential within the great Web of Life. Our wounding gives us the opportunity to transcend our human frailties and to reach a space beyond this world—a numinous place of comprehension that goes beyond right and wrong, beyond victim and perpetrator.

> Out beyond ideas of wrongdoing and rightdoing,
> there is a field. I'll meet you there.
>
> When the soul lies down in that grass,
> the world is too full to talk about.
>
> Ideas, language, even the phrase each other
> doesn't make any sense.
>
> - Rumi[85]

The Web of Life

Paradoxically, as you let go, you receive what is truly yours!

- Donna DeNomme

By moving beyond the selective dichotomy of what appears to be radically opposite, the vastness of the cosmos opens to us. We see that we are one interactive piece of a grand design and that we affect the greater whole each day and in every way that we live our lives—by what happens to us and how we deal with what happens to us. What we say and do has direct repercussions, and even our very existence is meaningful to the overall balance. Some of us have forgotten about this interconnection within the great Web of Life and the fact that what we do, even when no one is looking, affects the rest of that grand scheme.

Surprisingly, the one person many of us try to hide from most of all is ourselves. There truly is nowhere to run and nowhere to hide within this finely interconnected system. We cannot escape ourselves within the essential Web of Life! Sooner or later, we will be forced to come full center, looking ourselves straight in the eyes.

A Gateway (Initiation) to Higher Consciousness

When we can truly meet ourselves full on, we can then open our perception of the opposites within ourselves, which allows us to further examine the memories of our trauma and wounding. This is not an easy or a simple task, and as I have said before, one that is often enhanced by working with a professional guide. Yet, no matter how hard we try, we can never escape the need for doing this important work—it will keep coming back around until we attend to it.

As we muster the courage to consider a fuller reality concerning the abuse, trauma, and wounding, we come home to ourselves and make peace with the ugliness that still lives inside of us, enabling it to grow into something useful, and in some cases, downright beautiful. We recognize not only what we see as bad, but also what might be useful, as we integrate these insights into the fullness of who we are. Through the effectiveness of the 8 *Keys to Wholeness*, we can access the beauty and the wisdom previously locked inside of us and rise to the higher calling that is beckoning us to go beyond the pain to what is essential.

We are told that Post-Traumatic Stress Disorder (PTSD), resulting from many forms of trauma, may follow some victims for the rest of their lives. The reoccurrence of difficult memories and disturbing sensations can be devastating to those who experience its snare. With all due respect to the suffering of others, I might suggest that we reframe our thinking of PTSD to Post-Traumatic Situational Discovery: where we choose to meet our wounding within a safe and supported container (often with the help of a trained professional), so that we might nurture ourselves through the trauma, learning from the lessons and the wisdom that the experience surely holds. For, as we have examined through the chakras and the 8 *Keys to Wholeness*, every experience does hold meaning, especially our most challenging ones. Then, we can follow PTSD (Post-Traumatic Situation Discovery) with PTG (Post-Traumatic Growth), which may become the impetus for valuable new aspects being integrated into our evolving human development leading us ultimately to realize the greatest aspirations of our soul.

The suffering of our wounds is not the final destination. In the same manner that each of us has a unique and personal experience of birth when we come into this world, each piece of our personal history contributes to the birth of our becoming.

We can stay stuck in our wounds, spinning in cycles of bitterness and suffering or perpetuating abuse patterns that wound and rewound or we can shift and move to something more productive and more pleasant. As we rearrange the way we think about trauma as a static occurrence that happened to us, and instead view it through an expanded understanding of its contribution to our soul evolution, the lingering impact of the experience changes.

Did trauma ruin your life, or was there some aspect of it that provided an opportunity for you, perhaps developing one or more of those gems you discovered in the treasure chest found in Key #3? Even if you cannot fathom that any part of what you sustained could be remotely viewed as good or useful, can you accept that the aftermath is your chance to rise above the wounding into those parts of you that still long to express in the world? Powerful universal forces are at play, bringing you to the exact right point that pierces through the veil of illusion of separation, isolating you as a wounded victim.

It is not easy. To remain stuck in pain and fear, limited within a small scope of what is actually possible, may sometimes seem like the best option because it is known. The familiar pool of turmoil is one that many of us simply tread water in, attempting to keep our heads barely peeking above the turbulent waters, gasping a few desperate breaths of air. The reality is that just beyond that oppressive pool is a vast ocean of potential, simply awaiting our discovery of it.

When we become stuck in our wound, we miss the most important part of the equation— that it was initiatory. These experiences bring us to places we otherwise would not have accessed and help us accomplish tasks we might otherwise have not achieved. In spite of their horror, or perhaps because of it, abuse and trauma have the capacity to draw forth the very best parts of who we are at our core essence. If we can release the need to see what happened as simply bad or as only the tragedy that they are our lives, then we can open to their greater reflection.

I have found that the most fluid piece in this journey of transformation is what is within me—this is where I found the power to shift. And when I seized the courage to feel the intensity of my most difficult feelings, I was able to move into and through them to the other side, accessing a more empowered self.

Like the butterfly's becoming, our process of metamorphosis may literally feel like a complete dissolving of the old self, a death of sorts that allows us to emerge with wings to soar to new heights. Our inner journey blesses our outer lives. In my case, intense abuse caused a transpersonal crossing, offering a perspective that most likely would not have developed through typical childhood experiences. I was shown the way over an etheric bridge, allowing access to soothing information and support from other realms. My abuse opened a hyper-dimensional portal, through which the altar candle and my spiritual guides illuminated the way, the spirit bird became the vehicle of transport, and my young self embraced the journey as a means of escape from the cruelty of what was happening to me. I emerged into the grace of my right-to-be on this Earth, inseparable from my innate connection with the Divine. And through the ever-present mentoring of my guides, and the modalities and teachings they have directed me toward, I have continued to reconfirm that earlier understanding, developing a much-needed sense of personal empowerment.

Renaming whatever happened to us as useful and initiatory elevates it to its rightful status, bringing forth an authentic spiritual resonance that assigns meaningful purpose to something that in many cases would otherwise be intolerable. Our suffering offers a greater dimension of healing, as well as ascending portals of growth and enlightenment. This wounding is unavoidable, as it is an inescapable piece of our human experience, and although the content may differ, each one of us makes the treacherous journey. Each one feels pain, and everyone's pain matters.

Ultimately the question is this:

"Will your wounding destroy you, or will it empower you?"

Individual Healing affects the Collective

Although the specifics of your wounding may be uniquely yours, the healing of it is a collective contribution. Like individual air purifiers, we are able to clear a small part of the collective sludge, opening the creative field for a greater human expression. Our personal trauma is one expression of the greater collective suffering, and so, as we muster the courage to face our own trauma, that healing also provides a blueprint for expansion into the world. This is why it is so dramatically important for each person to do her own healing. As we heal, we help heal others. As we remember who we are and remember our truest connection, we can cooperatively help each other and our planet.

You are not alone in doing this important work—angels, mentors, and guides are here to assist you in this necessary process, and when you are ready for it, they will make themselves known to you. Ultimately, recognizing the fragments within you and uniting them is your individual task, and recognizing the external fragments in the outer world in order to heal that external separation is our collective task. Healing is your birthright . . . and it may also very well be your responsibility.

Who we are is shown by how we live—our words and actions are the true colors of our character. And your character is your most precious treasure, for hopefully, it is the expression of who you are authentically. You cannot escape the consequences of your attitude and actions because it is contributes to the overall expression of your life.

As each one of us does our own personal healing, we help to heal our outer, collective experience, and that outer experience then circles back around adding to our healing. We continue to evolve onward and upward in a reciprocally beneficial spiral pattern of ever-expanding, ever-reaching growth.

And as we heal, we can offer a hand to others, helping them with their changes, too. Because we recognize that our good is someone else's good, as theirs is ours, we do not need to hoard our gifts, attempting to keep them for ourselves; instead, having a genuine desire to share them in an ever-expanding generosity of spirit that often translates into serving others. As we personally refine our contribution, we give more and receive more, navigating the curves of that symbiotic personal /collective spiral. Instead of the constrictive, diminishing, and isolating downward spiral of victimhood, we are now on the expansive upward spiral of transformation.

Crown Healing: we are all in this together

How can we support each other? As a healer and a coach, I believe that this is a central question, because we can never really "fix" someone by trying to remedy their situation or ease their turmoil. What we think we see in any given moment is not the full complexity of a person's experience. If we rush in and try to rescue them from what may appear to be a difficult or painful transition, we, in fact, might prolong their pain. If that experience is necessary for them in some way, contributing to their development, "saving" them will actually require that they recreate or prolong the challenge in a different form, in order to glean the value of the lesson! So in a sense, projecting ourselves into someone else's mix as a directing influence actually impedes their overall progress. Life is too short to pull someone off course—it is much more supportive to allow others the necessary space to navigate their own directions, supporting them by believing that they are on a valuable life path. Knowing there is meaning and purpose in terms of personal growth and soul evolution provides patience for all of life's experiences.

This does not mean that we turn our backs on those in pain. Of course, we can be helpful and in some cases, even quite pivotal to someone else's healing. Certainly we can offer observations or suggestions, which is very different than trying to project our ideas of what we think should happen. The very best supporter does not superimpose her own choices, but rather walks with the ones in need, holding the belief that they are moving in a positive direction. At times, a supporter may also see the value of what is happening and the positive movement that is occurring, even when the one enmeshed in the difficulty or turmoil cannot. The supporter can then literally "hold the vision" of what is possible; knowing that in spite of how it looks, the healing can occur.

At other times, we may mirror back to someone something that appears to be missing or is hidden deep within them. As they hear or see it externally, reflected through our words or actions, there is a resonance that encourages them to accept that insight as their own. Such was the case with the unexpected impact of a comment made by my friend, Carl Studna, a gifted, world-renowned photographer with the ability to see through a clear personal lens.

Carl is a sensitive individual who shared that he had "some grief that was held in comfort and safety."[86] He continued saying, "It's now time to expand." I had never really looked at it that way, but I knew, in the moment that his words penetrated right through me, that he spoke my truth. I realized that, all things considered, this was the core of what kept me from speaking about my abuse all these years. My grief was safely locked within me—a place I could control—and it terrified me to think about exposing it to others with an unknown and uncontrollable result. Yet, it was time for me to face my deepest fear of speaking the whole truth out loud for all to hear.

At the same meeting, Reverend Barry Ebert, our beloved youth minister, offered one of his original songs. In part, the words are:

> Will you stand in the fire with me and help me hold my ground?
> And if my courage fails, and I start to run, turn me back around.
> Will you stand in the fire with me and open your heart with mine?
> I've never been down in such darkness before. It feels bigger than me this time.
> I'm not asking you for answers for all of these questions, or words to ease my mind.
> I just need somebody to listen sometimes, and I will pay you back in kind.[87]

What we all need most of all is simply to know that someone else cares. We need people who can stand with us in our pain, without trying to fix it so they can feel better. Each one of us has access to appropriate answers for ourselves. In spite of the appearance of trauma or chaos, when you are supporting someone else, the most important thing is your willingness to show up, with love, and stand with someone in the heat of their transformational flame.

In Key #1, you created a list of those people who could support you. Now, take the time to brainstorm a list of people whom you can support. Jot a few words about the pain or the turmoil that you think they are experiencing and a few ideas about how you might help.

- If you know someone who is in the midst of healing, perhaps even "the dark night of the soul," now is a good time to pause and give him or her a phone call or a visit to offer your support through a listening ear, a strong shoulder, or a gentle embrace.
- Often something simple, like going for a walk by the river or sitting together over a cup of tea or coffee, can mean a world of difference to someone going through a difficult time.

- If someone you know is in a life-threatening situation, every effort must be taken to keep that person safe.
- Still, the ultimate principle is the same. We each have a distinct life path filled with a variety of lessons leading us to our greater yet-to-be.

- How can you "stand in the flame" with those on your list? Your doing so not only helps them, but also reinforces your ability and strength to heal your own wounds.

Each one of your acts affect the threads in the eternal Web of Life. No action is too small to create a positive pattern that follows it. As proposed through the Butterfly Effect, a component of Chaos Theory, complex and unpredictable results may occur when we put forth a solitary effort. The description of this phenomenon is based on the idea that the fluttering of a butterfly's wings in China can affect the weather patterns in New York City!

Even if we never know a person who is being taken advantage of, his or her trauma, in some way touches us. No man, woman, or child is an island unto themselves. As we recognize the suffering of others, as well as looking at our own darkness, the collective consciousness is uplifted through the interconnected Web of Life. For the ultimate worth of our journey is when, in healing our own wounds or in supporting others with their wounding, we in turn create a greater ripple effect, like the butterfly's wings in China. Such is the intention of the shaman and the healer, the spiritual guide, and the coach.

7th Key to Wholeness: recognizing and living from oneness

As we ascend,

we gain consciousness of the more subtle aspects of our being

and begin to connect with all that is.

~ Madisyn Taylor[88]

We have explored many aspects of recognizing our Oneness and living in alignment with that understanding. There is one nuance that is often missed by those who have encountered great difficulty or horrendous trauma. We may have been left with a sense of being "less than," "not good enough," spoiled, or tainted in some way. Recognizing Oneness is partially about realizing our own importance in the overall scheme of life. We see that each piece of the puzzle is necessary and therefore precious to the whole.

Every detail of your story is significant, even when it seems pointless. And no matter how alone you may feel, you are always connected to all-there-is. What you do with your unique experiences matters, because it impacts others through the Web of Life. Every day, you are presented with the opportunity of how to deal with experiences you have had and the residual thoughts and emotions they left behind. Will you remain stuck in what you have been told or led to believe? Will you accept the limitations that have been put upon you? Or will you choose the direction of your own path and walk in the integrity of what you desire?

Circle of Appreciation

One way to cultivate a personal sense of peace and happiness and grow what is good in life is through the simple practice of appreciation. We turn our focus to what we like and why we like it. Some days this may be quite difficult, because finding anything in the midst of challenge or despair can be quite a stretch. But wherever you are and whatever is going on in your life, there is something or someone you can be pleased to know!

Create a Gratitude List

- Start small and acknowledge everything you can think of by recording it.
- Or make a collage with pictures cut from newspaper or sketches that you draw representing all the things you love in life.
- Remember to include what you appreciate about yourself. List the ways in which you are a gift to the world! How is the world better because you exist?
- Note three things you would like to eat, see, or do today. Choose three things that help you love your life!

Living from the truth of the 7th Key enables you to learn to truly love life and live it to the fullest, as you draw previously stagnant inner expressions forward, allowing them to make their way in the world. Express your core beauty and see the beauty in others, and believe in what is possible, even when situations are difficult or challenging. When you possess great hope that you are evolving toward wholeness, you can tap into the great perfection of the Universe, the Great Om, and realize that life truly is a glorious adventure!

Gratitude unlocks the fullness of life.

It turns what we have into enough, and more.

It turns denial into acceptance, chaos to order, confusion to clarity.

It can turn a meal into a feast, a house into a home, a stranger into a friend.

Gratitude makes sense of our past, brings peace for today,

and creates a vision for tomorrow.

~ Melody Beattie[89]

Breathe slowly, in and out, for three or four breath cycles. See that familiar red ray of the first power center grounding you with the earth beneath you, the orange ray of the second power center invigorating your creative potential, the yellow ray of your third center bringing meaning and purpose to your life, and the green hue of your heart essence blessing everything you do. You see the familiar blue ray of the Throat Chakra supporting your personal integrity to speak and live truth and the deep indigo of the 3rd Eye Chakra emanating from your forehead, like a guiding light, pointing the way toward your rightful path. Now, imagine the luminescent white of the Crown Chakra as you speak the following affirmative blessing with assurance and gratitude:

The world is my teacher, and I learn my lessons well! I rise to sacred wholeness, recognizing my oneness with the expression found in all there is. I have a deep relationship with my life's true purpose, moving beyond ego and ego wounding to my Higher Self. I open to know and trust my own wisdom, believing that truth speaks to me and through me, because I recognize myself as a spiritual being having a human experience. I am grateful for the many blessings I receive today, and in the spirit of the Great Om, I know and celebrate my Oneness with all that is before me and within me and in every facet of my Life!

8th Key

Radiate Your Evolving Essence
for True Transformation!

The call of our time is to transform old sludge into its new potential!

~ Donna DeNomme

When I peer into the pitch black of my own wounding, at first I see nothing. After some time and consideration, I eventually discover bountiful shards of great light penetrating the dark stain with unexpected illumination. And with the personal in-sight found by moving in and through my own darkness, I claim a destined power to bring forth healing change.

Within the disorientation of seeming chaos, I bump into a new and heightened order. When I connect with the Cosmic Christ Consciousness and the Buddha Path, I am able to creatively weave the divine in and through my thoughts, words, and actions. The Seat of the Soul supports me in this important mission to become a conduit for love, compassion, and mercy.

I explore ways to share the very best of who I am and who I might be, as I learn to love myself. The expression of my evolving Soul Essence offers a strong sense of inner peace. Conflicts and inner turmoil resolve as I embrace an expanded understanding of my karmic ideal and rise to the evolution of my life.

As we have examined the seven primary physical chakras and their seven keys to wholeness, we have discovered that each key could be used to open a doorway previously restricted or perhaps closed to us—in some cases even walled off! Opening those transformational portals exposed parts of ourselves that we have needlessly abandoned or dismissed. By engaging the help of each of our chakras, we can open these energetic channels for true and lasting healing.

The 8th and final key is available through the interaction of a synergistic triad of chakras: the Soul Star Chakra, the Earthstar Chakra, and the High Heart Chakra. The Soul Star is about five inches to two feet above the Crown Chakra. Its counterpart, the Earthstar is about one to two feet below the soles of the feet, and the High Heart Chakra is found in the collarbone or thymus area between the heart and the throat. The High Heart is particularly pivotal for abuse survivors as it relates to speaking our truth, seasoned with our deepest, truest heart essence—tempering the painful harshness of our experience with the comfort of expanded understanding. Utilizing the energy of the High Heart enables us to connect the lower chakras with the upper chakras through a bridge of love and compassion. Joining that High Heart with the upper and the lower Star Chakras provides a strong axis for empowered living.

Accessing the energy of the etheric chakra in our triad, the Soul Star Chakra or the Star Chakra, allows us to more intimately connect with the vastness of the cosmos recognized and accessed in Key #7. This final Key offers a direct connection with the Christ Consciousness or Buddha Understanding taking our awareness of Oneness even further. Having paused at the intersection of the opposites and understanding that Spiritual Essence, the vital Universal Life Force Itself, is not just what we perceive as "good," but rather unfolds through all of our life experiences offers meaning to even the most unconceivable wound. Personal knowledge and acceptance of our divine oneness with all things provides the ability to relate from a broader and more inclusive perspective. Tapping the wisdom of this chakra quite literally asks us to "rise above" our human condition and realize the ultimate value of our interrelations with others and with the physical world all around us.

We are called to release any need to re-enact our hardships through repetitive or lashing out behaviors, and instead are inspired to open to a clearer, brighter expression. This chakra enlists us to manifest higher truths directly through our thoughts, words, and actions. Sparked by the Source of life and its harmonious frequencies, the Soul Star enables us to unlock behaviors that are for our highest good as well as for the good of the whole, as we activate those parts of ourselves that stretch into our evolving personal and collective wholeness.

Within this center is the memory of divine love, spiritual compassion, and spiritual wisdom. Our contact with the heightened vibration of the Soul Star Chakra encourages us to embrace the evolving purpose of our personal history and of life itself. As we rise above the density of our human limitations to encounter the illumination of the enlightenment found here, we discover that we are at the gateway to spiritual understanding. We encounter the secret to our next phase of human evolution—the promise that we can move beyond our wounding, through lasting healing, and into our Divine Right Wholeness, the absolute truth of our Higher Self.

Developing Our Night Vision

> Shining light into the darkness illuminates Truth.
> As we feel, so we heal—lifetimes!
>
> – Donna DeNomme

Remembering that the word shaman literally means "one who sees in the dark,"[90] we recognize that the shaman uses her ability to see in the darkness, so she may help to heal a physically or psychically sick person. What if each of us took on the responsibility for looking into our own darkness in order to secure our own healing?

Joseph Campbell proposed the idea that we each embark on a hero's journey in our lifetime with challenges and successes along the way; the goal being to "bring back the gold"—the insight and wisdom that can be useful to our family and community. Marion Woodman warns us that "bringing the treasure back from the underworld into life is always the most hazardous task in the fairytale."[91] That is because there is so much at stake—what we carry has the potential to create change, and in some cases, to be an important catalyst for both a personal and collective shift. Bringing back the treasure is about sharing the gold of our character.

As previously noted, our words and actions have consequences, contributing to the downward or upward spiral of our life expression. The vibrations of our actions circle back around with the ability to catapult downward or upward movement through the events in our lives. By utilizing the inspirational energies of the Soul Star Chakra, we open our emotional channels for true happiness and the potential of a greater and greater evolution of life fulfilled.

This is not to say that we assume a Pollyanna-type attitude, whitewashing the difficulty of the outer world or our own experiences while ignoring what appears to be the harsh reality of them. It simply means that we perceive through our highly developed night vision, seeing through what is light and also through what is dark. We observe what appears to be real, and we search for its truest message.

This also does not mean that there are never immediate reactions that divert us from the expression of our core Self. We are human after all and prone to such behavior! But we choose not to live in those places of limitation, rigid judgment, or destruction, instead remaining open to the fluid synchronicities of life that lead us to a greater expression of our humanity.

By looking through the lens of the healer, we open to the further possibility of what might be useful within even the worst of traumas. Sometimes the potential of what has been gained strains the limits of what we consider logical, but the underlying truth stands that we can change for the better. We are reminded that the lasting effect of our lives is not what happens to us, but what we do with those challenges. By our willingness to turn ourselves inside out and explore even the most painful parts of what we hold, we allow the innate beauty of what is buried to seek expression.

Once we have examined various perspectives and gathered as many facets of understanding as possible, then we can make conscious and clear choices as to how to proceed. Instead of living from a reactive stance, we navigate through life with purposeful actions. Our unique personality and the character we develop become the footprints we eternally leave in the changing sands of life's memory . . . . Venture into the innermost parts of yourself and the outermost reaches of your potential, so you may bring forth greater healing and a life beyond what you may even imagine.

And furthermore, somewhere along the discovery of this 8th Key, the ultimate motivation becomes clear: it is not because of what we might "get" that we alter our behaviors. It is because of the value of what we might give. As we discover appropriate ways to express our golden aspects, life becomes rich with opportunities to bring forth the very best parts of who we are and who we might grow to be. When we give our gifts without attachment, we relieve the negative stress necessary to hold the tension required to push things down inside us or strain to manipulate situations in the exact direction that we desire. We truly relax and let go into the flow of life, trusting in our ability to handle its twists and turns. And consequently, our open and selfless altruism, which contributes to the outer world, also blesses us from the inside out!

Remember Demeter and Persephone from the 2nd Key? You can reread it, if necessary, to have the story fresh in your mind, because there is much more to that story! After her abduction, Persephone began to help those who were stuck between the worlds find safe passage by moving completely into the Underworld. She knew the path by heart from her own journey back and forth, and she used that information to help others. Persephone served a worthy and respected role during her time with Hades and became a powerful Goddess, far different from the innocent maiden who was snatched from the sunny garden. Here is the story from Hades' perspective:

> she was there, playing in the fields
> and i simply plucked her as if she were a flower
> delicately soft and sweet;
> innocent in her youth.

she, herself, gathered the flowers

with an appreciation for their beauty,

and i, unto her, did the very same.

the earth opened to receive her,

as she did to me;

each mirroring the other, with a penetration

that brought forth the new.

for to ever remain as the maiden

happy at play in the field,

would have denied her the opportunity

to become queen—

a possibility

held within her own darkness.

the shadow of the daughter-denied

was the woman-embraced.

i took her below

and made her my treasured queen;

all riches i gave freely to her.

and she, to me,

offered companionship

and the beauty of her sweet form next to mine.

ours may not be a match made in heaven, but it is surely divine!

you humans desire a love

that basks only in the light of day

yet true love

moves into the darkness of what you wish not to see.

walking hand-in-hand through an unknown land,

being open to what may create anew;

for it is within the chaos

and the emptiness of the void,

that all else might come forth . . . .

it is here that one claims her unexpected crown.

so like persephone, you must fall not onto

the earth, but into it,

whether by choice

or by the gods and fate itself.

to become completely naked

is to discover a hidden wealth.

perhaps, like her, you may go kicking and screaming,

longing for what you have left behind,

missing the cradle of your mother's arms.

remember to be like persephone

who,

in keeping with the company of her own terror

found her true self—

born of the underworld—

and her willingness

to taste its sweetness.

seven tiny seeds of pomegranate nectar

bound her securely.

she was forever wed to the underworld,

and to me.

my queen performed great deeds,

which would have gone undone,

if not for her.

she brought a strength and knowing

far beyond her youth,

as she quickly grew

into the wise woman

who was she.

and although i long for her whenever she is gone,

i know with certainty that she will return,

for without me now,

each and every time need be,

she finds the path,

knowing her own way . . .

home.[92]

We can access our greater purpose, our soul mission, by meeting the archetypal challenges that arise within us. We reveal our soul essence in all of its multi-faceted layers as we evolve through our life experiences. By working them through to a point of insight, they provide us with an illumined lens of discovery, leading to enlightened thought and transpersonal growth. Let's encourage each other to bring back this precious wisdom held within us or hidden within the difficulty of life's strife. Recognize, right now, in this moment that all of life conspires for your healing and your soul evolution![93]

Infinite Promise

Eight is a powerful number. In many traditions eight signifies the potential to balance the material and immaterial worlds. The number eight visually and energetically holds the promise of infinity—an eternal life that circles back around upon itself for heightened evolution.

The counterpart of the Soul Star Chakra is the Earthstar Chakra, found about 12 – 24 inches below the feet. The Soul Star is often seen as luminescent white, shimmering with its eternal light and its earth twin, the Earthstar Chakra, appears as a very dark brown or black. Through this chakra we are called to ground our in-sight and inspiration into concrete words and actions that take shape and form in the physical world. We transport what is divine through our human experiences, acting as a bridge between heaven and earth. In this respect, tragedies and traumas have the ability to connect you with your soul and to bring that luminous soul truth into your mundane daily world.

The lower Earthstar also helps us to access karmic influences, as well as familial lineages, which contribute to our evolving personalities. As these often unconscious tendencies surface into our conscious awareness, they can further develop within our embrace. The Universal Soul also provides seemingly chance discoveries (often called synchronicities) for re-membering—reclaiming forgotten or disowned parts of ourselves and integrating them back into our core. In some cases, we may need to re-pattern either our familial influences or our disowned aspects in order to find their usefulness, but the essential kernel is recognizing something that was there all along.

Such was the case with learning to understand the word "victim" in a different way, accepting its truth as my own. By embracing the horrible secret of my abuse and freeing the wounded one, I was able to further cleanse her of the evil harshness that was done to her. With clear intention to find further meaning and healing, I have consecrated her pain with purpose. In the light of day, she now basks in the forgotten sun, soaking in its vital nutrients and growing strong with life. I am integrating her into my health and wholeness. In further developing my understanding, the wounding did not change, but its capacity of meaning did evolve, providing significant worth. I am still experiencing the ripples of that profound acceptance!

Although particular moments may be quite important, our becoming most often does not occur in the flash of a single moment. Evolution is not found in the location of a predetermined goal to be attained, but rather over the course of a lifetime journey leading into a distant horizon dawning with enlightenment.

Marion Woodman says,

> Integrating an initiation can become a lifetime task.
> And while most of it remains in the secret mysteries of the individual,
> some of it belongs to the universal soul
> that is striving to become conscious in each one of us.[94]

Our personal traumas crack us open, so we can move through them into a space of compassion with the indisputable awareness of something greater. It is a powerful stance to reach down into the deepest parts of ourselves and touch tender wounds that have remained locked inside of us, accepting the task of healing. And healing at the root is profound and lasting, bringing forth healing on all levels: body, mind, and spirit.

Through the multifaceted vibrations of the lofty Soul Star Chakra and the practical and grounded strength of the Earthstar Chakra, we are able to move deeply within our own potential, where we can see the karmic or soul purpose of our suffering. What were we supposed to learn? And can we carry that message back? Like shamans returning from the underworld, we can create that bridge between spirit and matter by hearing and listening to the voice of our souls.

When we find the purpose of our wounds, it elevates them to the respectful status they deserve. The suffering, the turmoil, the despair is no longer just trauma, but has a significant role in our becoming who we were meant to be, in realizing our soul purpose. Our divine mission is not to be a victim; the value is found on the other side of that limited identity.

What is your true purpose? Through the vibration of the Earthstar, the 8th Key opens our awareness to grasp specific soul agreements (or spiritual contracts) that affect life experience and life purpose. We have agreed to walk our divine assignment, to share our divine potential, and to follow our divine inspiration. Through the soles (souls) of our feet, we shape our divine understanding into form as we learn to consciously co-create our lives. We can contribute our truest Self with the potential to bring forth great change . . . . And we witness it all with an acceptance and understanding of the part it plays in the greater scheme of life. Your life can make a difference. You are an integral piece of the momentum of life unfolding.

Crossing the Etheric Bridge: hope-filled healing

The third chakra utilized in the 8th Key is the High Heart Chakra found between the heart and the throat in the collarbone or thymus area. The color of this chakra is often seen as aqua or teal, depending on the strength of the heart (green) and the throat (blue) at any particular moment. As outlined in Key #4, tapping into the deeper essence of our essential heart can be instrumental to healing, and when it is combined with the powerful energy found in Key #5, speaking our truth, the results can be astounding. The High Heart enables us to further traverse the boundaries that seemingly limit our human emotions.

There is a world between the worlds, one that is as real as the outer world of the senses and the intellect. This world is not of our fantasy, but rather is an "imaginal" realm, meaning that it goes beyond our physical reality into the world of images. Information from this realm may push at our notions of what we refer to as "common sense," inviting us to stretch into something beyond our human intellect. Henry Corbin calls this the *mundis imaginalis*, saying it "contrasts with the order of reality," in that its sensory information may not necessarily make logical sense on the worldly plane. This is the kind of information we can sense with the High Heart; it is felt when we simply "know" what is true (or the opposite, when we sense that something is not true). Tapping into the *mundis imaginalis* enables us to access information that conveys more than what we know intellectually and more than what we have learned through our direct experience. This knowledge is seasoned with a divine glimmer of the potential that can be drawn into our physical reality—these are the visions of what is yet-to-be.

Encountering the *mundis imaginalis* is not a movement from one place to another, but rather a shifting that happens within us. This master journey develops our relationship between the inner, invisible, and esoteric realm, and its counterpart, the outer, visible, and exoteric.[95] The *mundis imaginalis* is also the dimension that enables us to truly understand our oneness with all things, because as we journey inside of ourselves to explore those inner realities, paradoxically, we often find ourselves on the outside, in the vastness of the cosmos, interconnected and harmonious with all things. We learn the significance of the relationship between our individual, inner realities and our outer experiences.

Tom Cheetham describes this process as a "spiritual birth [that] frees the soul from its entrapment in and subordination to an alien and external world."[96] Historically, it has been the shamans who traversed this terrain to access its knowledge and bring the wisdom back to the people. Ours is an age when so many of us are being called to recognize and attempt this journey of piercing the illusionary and elusive veil between the worlds. We can shift our usual perception to encompass so much more, becoming more fully awakened to the multi-dimensional realities all around us. There are so many truths just beyond our fingertips waiting to be touched, felt, and claimed. Listening and seeing with the capacity of the High Heart accesses these gems.

When Jesus visited my healing room while I was working with my students, I assumed that He was there for them. After all, I had not had a close relationship with Him since childhood. Although I was a very spiritual person, my personal beliefs did not embrace the teachings of the Church that had abused me. At this time of my life, I still harbored unconscious anger and probably even blamed Him for what they did to me in His name. But there is more to his loving visit . . . .

He comes once again, a few days later. I am one of several practitioners working around a massage table. We are all teachers, meeting for our monthly exchange. He appears behind my left shoulder, those astoundingly loving eyes peering right into me. I feel a warmth and appreciation like no other, one I'd like to bask in forever.

Without a word, He purposely steps forward, moving into my body. As I feel the loving gentleness of his hands reaching through mine, they touch me from the inside, reaching into every place within and without, reaching into the deepest parts of me.

In the same exact moment that they are touching me with such tenderness and healing, they also become my hands. His touch reaches out through me, as we seem to melt into One physical expression.

In that instant, I know, without any doubt, my divine Wholeness.

His profound acceptance healed the deepest aching of my broken heart. In those brief moments, walls within me crumbled as I opened to fresh vistas before me. Within me I found a personal safety and deep inner peace as I realized that He had never really abandoned me. My heart, previously held captive, was released to explore newfound freedom and dance with great joy.

8th Key to Wholeness: radiate your evolving essence

This is the message of the lofty Star Chakra and the grounded Earthstar Chakra, drawn through the profound and essential love of the High Heart in the triad of our 8th Key. It is from this elevated space that we might truly radiate the beauty of our evolving essence. And when we ground that evolved essence through the choices in our relationships with others and our pursuits in life, then we radiate our evolving essence into true transformation. We step forward with divine grace.

We Shift from Being a Victim and Embrace Life as a Healer.

The 8th Key allows us to move fully through our wounding into its righteous healing so we can radiate our personal illumination for the benefit of all. We open our arms wide to share the illumination of our High Heart in every direction, seasoned with the enlightened energy of the Soul Star, and grounded with the solid energy of the Earthstar. We shine our radiance into the world!

Rainbow Healing

Imagine the beautiful variations of a brilliant rainbow

stretching across a vast blue sky . . . .

~ Donna DeNomme

We have acknowledged and connected with the enlivened energy of ten of our personal chakras. As we stretch into the wisdom and the power of this final key, we experience the interconnection between the varying hues of all of the chakras, realizing that within us we embody the fullness of the rainbow and its potential for healing and transformation.

In many wisdom traditions, a rainbow is a symbol of great hope, an "emblem of promise." Judy Garland as Dorothy in *The Wizard of Oz* sang so beautifully about a land she heard about in a lullaby, "somewhere over the rainbow." Yet, we need not travel into the sky or the heavens to find a sense of wonder and peace despite our troubles. Like Dorothy, taking an unknown path leads you right back into your life, because *there is no place like home* and you carry your true home inside of you wherever you go. Garland croons about a place over the rainbow where "dreams that you dare to dream" really can come true. Know that there is an infinite and wondrous potential of life available, and draw on that goodness right here, right now.

No matter what the unrest, there is an underlying calm.

No matter what the emotional trauma, there is an inner peace.

No matter what the apparent discord, there is a basic harmony.

No matter what the physical imbalance, there is perfect, complete healing.

No matter how dark it might seem, there is ever-present, ever-nurturing Light.

Look within to your own deeply rooted understanding of peace, harmony, and total well-being.

Allow the fertile seed to burst forth into creative life expression, blooming with multi-colored vibrant beauty, for all to see!

~ Donna DeNomme, 1992

We recognize the importance of our individuality, the gifts and personality traits which make us truly unique. Like a rainbow, each of the individual colors is distinct, yet its edges are not separate or necessarily even clearly defined. Each ray is interconnected in the magnificence of that beautiful arching hoop stretching through the sky; yet each aspect possesses its own unique radiance, contributing to the fullness of the rainbow expression. No one is less or more important than the next. With the understanding of this interrelatedness, we know that just as all the rays of the rainbow have value, each person and each situation does as well.

Our call is to bloom with multi-colored vibrant beauty, honoring the various rays of our expression, and embracing the vast reach of our entire rainbow personality. As we act as a part of the bridge to the divine, we can reveal our most miraculous abilities and truest dreams, transcending our human ideas of space and time and integrating them into the universal reality of the here and now. It is never too late to heal. It is never too late to grow into the person you were meant to be.

The prophecy of the Rainbow Warriors foretold through many wisdom traditions calls for us to be our own shamans, our own priests, and our own healers, in order to come together in harmony for the good of the planet. We look at the fullness of what was, and is, and then ask, "What else?" What is still longing to express through me? And how can I contribute to the multi-colored vibrant beauty of life? How can I support Mother Earth as well as Father Sky and all of the kingdoms on this precious planet? As we heal, we help to infuse the greater world healing.

Our Soul Imprints

There is not just one particular direction we must choose, but rather many variations on how we might live our lives. Our choices are often seasoned by the information contained within our Soul Imprint. Whether or not you believe in some predetermined destiny, it is fascinating to explore how and why we might encounter particular experiences. What part do they play in the bigger picture? Why did your particular experiences happen to you? And why are you reading my words at this exact time of your life?

Someone once asked if I ever felt "chosen." Have you ever felt that way? As if you were somehow chosen to live your most challenging experiences? Through them we develop particular pieces of our personalities, so to contemplate the idea that those experiences might have somehow been destined is, at the very least, an interesting consideration!

I acknowledge, with respect, the enormity of what you have been through and the significance of your pain. Please know that none of what I say is to discount what you have sustained. Abuse of any kind perpetrated by another person onto an adult or child, the pain of heartbreak or the loss of relationship, and the challenge of addictions or unhealthy behaviors are as varied and complex as each individual. In no way am I saying that transformation is easy. But it is essential. Through accepting your individual pieces as purposeful, you can see them as necessary to completing your own personal "puzzle" of life. Yours is a masterpiece, and whether or not you feel that you were chosen to experience your particular wounds, work the contours of their shape and size into harmony and balance with the rest of your core self, so you can properly place those pieces within the context of your bigger picture.

In your notebook or journal, record:

- Any trauma that still impacts you.
- Any trauma or wounding that you think no longer impacts you, but was significant.

- Take several days over a week's time and brainstorm a list of lessons learned and insights gleaned through these experiences. There is no need to separate out which wounding your wisdom originated with, as patterns often surface over a range of times. We learn and re-learn the same lesson until we really understand it and integrate it into our core selves.

- Place your writing aside for several weeks and then revisit it.

- Repeat the process without looking at your initial notes.
- Reread both entries.
- Reconnect with your list of support people, knowing that they are there to help you on your journey toward integration and wholeness.

The overall balance of life contains the contrast of both light and dark. We cannot completely perceive, until all is said and done, what will be our most transformative times. The darkest parts may provide the brightest gifts, in the same way that the brilliance of the stars seem illumined next to the darkness of the night sky. As the philosopher Friedrich Nietzsche says, "You must have chaos within you to be able to give birth to a dancing star!" With that illumination, may we each have the courage to embrace our darkest nights and our most confusing chaos in order to birth the brilliance held within us, so that we might offer it, in service, to uplift and enlighten the world. We can serve the greater whole of humanity simply by fully living our most complete life.

Together, we are expressing a new design—one that recognizes trauma in all of its forms as a significant, even essential, piece of our development. Our growing pains may seem almost unbearable; yet, the growth they possess is equal to or exceeds the pain, suffering, or emotional agony. Persevering through the achievement of their full maturity draws forth all that we have inside of us. The potential of our lives and the ability to develop into that fullness are quite literally within our reach in the sacred triad of the Soul Star chakra, the Earthstar chakra, and the High Heart chakra. The call of life is to rise to the task of utilizing those energies to elevate our human existence to more than it seems to be . . . .

Know that Divinity resides within you and expresses through your ability to stretch into what you can yet be. You are guided by the presence of Divine Wisdom, which knows the essential truth, so rest assured that you are on the "right" path as you embody the brilliance of the rainbow after the storm. Radiate your absolute beauty and the great magnificence of your evolving soul essence as you move through your human experiences, and you will create Heaven here on Earth.

Protective Chakra Meditation

Invite in the now-familiar image of the red cord of light moving through the base of your spine into the earth below you. See it connect with and activate the dark brown or black space of the Earthstar Chakra below you. The combination of these two chakras connecting with purpose is very powerful, and you feel a surge of energy and light grounding you into the very core of the earth, holding you securely in this physical plane. Breathe for a few cycles of conscious breath, in and out with ease and flow, as you celebrate the exchange of energy here: the earth claims you as her daughter and promises to hold you with a sturdy base, and you in exchange promise to protect Her for future generations.

Now see the orange hue of the Sacral Chakra connect with the red and the black as you embrace the creativity of your life. Know that in any given situation, you possess what is needed to navigate with and through the happenings of your life. Breathe. Imagine the vibrant yellow of the solar plexus again connecting with the downward flow, as you know and declare your significance and purpose here on earth. Know that your earth journey is one filled with choice, and dedicate yourself to living life as you wish it to be.

Follow the rainbow thread upwards now, as you connect with the beautiful rays of your own heart and drink of its healing green essence. Know the comfort and the safety of your own heart, as you promise to be gentle and loving with yourself through all of your changes. Breathe for several breaths in and out, savoring the sanctuary of this space . . . .

Move gently upward as you connect with the High Heart just above the heart and tap into its glorious aqua beauty. Know the presence of this place intimately, as you connect beyond your human capacity to that of the greater love, the Infinite Presence of Unconditional Love and Absolute Healing. Draw that memory forward and up, as you unite it with the blue of your throat center and the ability to speak your truth, as well as to speak beyond what you know as true. Open to the greater potential wishing to express through you.

Breathe. . . . As you move to join the healing indigo vibration of the 3rd Eye, which reawakens you to the insight and grace that you carry inside of you always, know who you are. Recognize an inner authority as your sacred guidance, knowing that no external source can ever override the internal Spiritual Source that speaks to you through your innermost knowing. Breathe as the rainbow blessing stretches to your uppermost limit of the violet Crown at the very top of your head, and know the intimacy of this space that connects you to All-There-Is and yet is so uniquely personal. Celebrate your divinity, which moves beyond worldly limitations as you recognize the eternal wholeness readily available to you.

Now breathe the connection of the entire rainbow cord: the black, the red, the orange, and the yellow, the green, the aqua, the blue, the indigo and the violet as they now stretch to greet the luminescent white hovering above your head. You pierce beyond the limiting veil of your human condition to accept your divine birthright as a child of life itself. You observe a subtle glimmer of the magnificent radiance available within this sacred space as you vow to fulfill the promise held within you.

Letting go of the need to remain locked in a sense of victimhood, you open to the possibility of further integrating your wounded self into the wholeness of your being, knowing that all parts of you have value in the overall scheme of life. You let go—and in letting go, you draw yourself closer.

As you continue to breathe with conscious and full breaths, you open to the fullness of life before you. You know and trust in your destiny, for it is beyond your wildest dreams. And in the quiet of this moment, with all parts of you united with promise and purpose, you fully accept the value of who you are, as you know your own Spiritual Divinity. Happiness washes over you with the sweetness of newfound hope and the release of the salty taste of your own tears. Life is waiting before you, and in this moment, your heart quickens with what is ahead.

From this moment on, in just one breath, in just one moment, you can return with your awareness to this place. You can become grounded and uplifted. You can remember who you are. You can connect with the Soul Star above you for enlightenment and the Earthstar below you for manifestation, as you filter all you say and do through the brilliance of your High Heart, which knows the truth of your being. It is from this place that you move forward, into further healing and soul evolution, as you live life with sweet happiness and great success.

The only story you have is your own. You can live it from a place of reluctantly taking what you "get," or you can seize the opportnity it presents in a way that enables you, through conscious choice and purposeful actions, to shape and reshape it. Embrace your powerful karmic destiny as you work through Universal archetypal patterns expressing through you, and rise to your fullest expression. As you work to master your own material, whether or not you share the details, you vibrationally contribute your precious treasure of meaning and insight to the collective good. Your life matters . . . . In the warm glow of the candle flame, I see who you are.

To make an end is to make a beginning . . . .
We shall not cease from exploration and the end of all our exploring will be to arrive
where we started and know the place for the first time.
~ T.S. Eliot[97]

Donna DeNomme is a role model for using life challenges as opportunities to propel oneself into an extraordinary life. Coming from a background of brutal sexual abuse, which led to rebellious adolescent gang affiliation, single motherhood, and state welfare, Donna knew first-hand how self-defeating life can be . . . . Until now, Donna has not disclosed the details of those times, but rather used them as a foundation for personal and professional empowerment. She believes the ultimate purpose is in our healing, not our wounding. Donna lives life with great enthusiasm, knowing that there is true insight and value in all of our experiences.

Donna is an author, speaker, conscious energy teacher, licensed spiritual coach, and ceremonial leader. She has a Bachelor's degree in Human Development and Family Studies from Cornell University, a Master's Degree in Engaged Humanities with an emphasis in Depth Psychology from Pacifica Graduate Institute, an advanced certification in Spiritual Coaching, and many years of training in alternative therapies and indigenous healing studies.

Donna has led innumerable women's groups, spiritual retreats, and other enrichment programs, and has released two meditation CD's, *Spinning the Light* and *Sacred Journey*. Donna's art is the creation of nurturing and supportive, richly charged environments that help to facilitate others as they explore, expand, and deepen their sense of self and their unique way of being in the world. Utilizing many modalities, some of which she professionally developed, Donna is a Master Success Coach and workshop facilitator with over 25 years of experience assisting others. She was voted Colorado's "Spiritual Health Guru" by the prestigious 5280 Magazine, for her unique approach to healing.

For more information on speaking, coaching, or ceremonial development, visit Donna's website at www.wildsuccess4you.com.

Books and Products

8 Keys Meditation CD (2014)

Guided meditations lead the listener through the discovery and activation of the 8 Keys.

Turtle Wisdom: Coming Home to Yourself (2007)

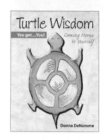

An endearing, award-winning book of guidance, gentle encouragement, and practical inspiration reminding you that you carry what is most precious and essential. A gift that says, "I believe in you!" Now being published in 8 countries.

Turtle Wisdom: Personal Illumination Cards (Satiama 2013)

Who says your spiritual journey can't be fun? Whimsically illustrated in full-color, this 44-card deck and guidebook will support both inexperienced and mature spiritual travelers on their personal development path.

Ophelia's Oracle: Discovering the Healthy, Happy, Self-Aware, and Confident Girl in the Mirror (2009)

Co-authored with storyteller Tina Proctor / for girls 10-16.
A delightful story girls' love, partnered with fun activities, beautiful illustrations, interviews, and inspirational poetry that parents and educators appreciate. OO has been used as confidence-building curriculum in schools. 15 Awards for Excellence!

Writing the Shadows (2014)

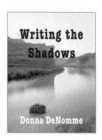

Guided processes and encouragement for writing about your most difficult experiences for personal exploration, enhanced understanding, and enlivened growth. May be used with Donna's online course.

Author Acknowledgements

So many people supported the release of this book through four years of writing and development. I am grateful to Carol Lowell, who first planted the seed for this project, and Gil and Danna Gray for their early encouragement.

I discovered that Pacifica Graduate Institute was the perfect place to start this writing. Exceptional teachers encouraged my personal and academic exploration, and the intimacy of a very small cohort of students furthered the opportunity to examine in detail what I had avoided most of my life. Research and writing completed for classes with Ana Mozol, Susan Rowland, Dara Marks, Safron Rossi, Maren Hansen, Paul Jones, Joan Abraham, and Jennifer Selig were especially important to this manuscript. I am also grateful for the caring guidance of my final project advisor, Cynthia King, who remained available to me after the completion of my degree to review this final version of my work.

With sincere appreciation to my cohort at Pacifica for their unwavering intellectual and emotional support: Christy Schumann, Linda King, and Tabatha Walters—thank you. Thanks also to our sister cohort who shared 18 months of our academic journey: Mandy Kruger, Bree Cogshell, Maria Luisa Diaz de Leon Zuloaga, Saundra Salyer, and William Mueller.

There were many points when I thought about abandoning this project altogether. Except for living through the experience of the abuse, this writing was the single most difficult task of my life. There were pivotal moments when an angel appeared in the form of someone I knew, who spoke the exact right words to keep me moving along. Heartfelt appreciation for Dianne Fresquez, Deborah Sandella, Cynthia James, Sue Loving, and Sue Lion—you are the godmothers of this book!

Due to the nature of this writing, I engaged the help of over 40 readers before my final edits. My thanks go out to all of you, especially: Janis Page, Michele Altieri, Deborah Sandella, Dianne Fresquez, Mary Jo Honiotes, Tina Proctor, Dennis Grogan, Rasamayi Turturici, Deb Klepsch, Carl Studna, Sherry Ray, Jeanne Belli, Trudy Welty, Fawn Germer, Anne Clark-Caya, and Cindy Cable.

I want to especially acknowledge those mentioned in the healing segments for your powerful contributions. And to all of you who work serving others in healing professions—you lift us up to more of who we might be . . . . To my spiritual and shamanic teachers, both seen and unseen: your beacons are the guiding light of my life.

My sincere appreciation to the New York Times best-selling writer Kathryn Harrison, who wrote the fictionalized *Thicker Than Water*, followed by her courageous non-fiction version, *The Kiss*. You are a fine example of the undying need for survivors to explore the best ways to tell the truth of what happened to them.

To my mother and father, who did the very best they could with what I gave them through all the unusual changes of my life: I love you, and I know that you love me.

To the rest of my family, thank you for sharing the journey with me. A special warm thanks to Uncle Hank and Aunt Kathy, devout Catholics, who have been especially supportive of my acknowledging the pain of my childhood experience.

To my roommate Dianne Fresquez who lived with this project day in and day out for four years—your support cannot be measured.

To the readers, thank you for your interest in this book. You are the reason I took the time to write it. I hope you find something of value here.

To Cara Cantarella, an exquisite editor, who notices the smallest detail, and with the shift of a word or a comma makes it sing—my deepest gratitude.

To my illustrator and graphic designer, Sue Lion, I so appreciate you creating the beautiful illustrations and helping with the nuts and bolts of bringing this project to completion. I am especially thankful for your steady hand on my shoulder all along the way, saying, "Donna, it is time . . . ."

And most of all, to my spiritual guides, the Guardian Council of Light: you have always been there for me. Thank you for giving me the choice . . . and leading me in the direction that provided the courage.

I love you!

End Notes and References Cited:

Introduction:

1. Marie-Louise von Franz, *Projection and Re-collection in Jungian Psychology: Reflections of the Soul*, Open Court, 1995, p.141 with permission.
2. "Opening to the Potential of the New Year," centering meditation, facilitated by Cynthia James, January 2010. www.cynthiajames.net.
3. Excerpt from *The Book of Symbols: Reflections on Archetypal Symbolism*, Taschen, 2010 in the essay on Chakras. Published with kind permission from The Archive for Research in Archetypal Symbolism (ARAS), www.aras.org.

Chapter One:

4. With permission from *The Way to Rainy Mountain* by Momaday, N. Scott ©1976 University of Mexico Press.
5. Dr. Ana Mozol "Trauma and Dreams," Dreamwork, Fall 2010, lecture with permission.
6. Judith Herman, *Trauma and Recovery: The Aftermath of Violence* New York: Basic Books, 1992, p.38. Reprinted with permission.
7. Elizabeth Goudge (1900 - 1984) from Green Dolphin Street Coward McCann, Inc, 1944.
8. Note: names or identies have been changed when the individuals involved where not attainable for granting permission or when necessary to protect their privacy.
9. Coleman Barks, "Out Beyond" reprinted with permission from *A Year with Rumi: Daily Readings* and *The Essential Rumi*, HarperCollins, 2006.
10. Reprinted from *Sophia: The Feminine Face of God* (2011) by Karen Speerstra with permission of Divine Arts, Studio City, California. www.divineartsmedia.com.
11. From *Masks of God: Primitive Mythologies* by Joseph Campbell, copyright © 1959, 1969, renewed © 1987 by Joseph Campbell. Used by permission of Viking Penguin, a division of Penguin Group (USA) LLC.
12. Don Oscar Miro-Quesada. Ceremonial description and foundation information. The Heart of the Healer Foundation (THOTH), www. heartofthehealer.org or refer to Lessons in Courage: Peruvian Shamanic Wisdom for Everyday Life by Bonnie Glass - Coffin, Ph.D and Don Oscar Miro-Quesada. Rainbow Ridge Publishing, 2013.
13. Don Oscar Miro-Quesada. Personal conversation, September 12, 2010.
14. "The Miracle of Mindfulness" by Thich Nhat Hanh. Copyright © 1975, 1976 by Thich Nhat Hanh. Preface and English translation Copyright © 1975, 1976, 1987 by Mobi Ho. Reprinted by permission of Beacon Press, Boston.

Chapter Two

15. Janet Morley from *All Desires Known: Third Edition*. Used with permission from Church Publishing Incorporated, New York, NY.
16. Thomas P. Doyle, "Clericalism and Catholic Clergy Sexual Abuse," in *Predatory Priests, Silenced Victims: The Sexual Abuse Crisis and the Catholic Church* edited by Mary Gail Frawley-O'Dea and Virginia Goldner. The Analytic Press, 2007, p.154 reprinted with permission.
17. Ibid, p. 155.
18. Kathleen M. Dwyer, "Surviving is what I know; living is what I am learning" in *Predatory Priests, Silenced Victims*, Frawley-O'Dea/Goldner, p.103 – 109 reprinted with permission.
19. Kate Osborn *Disgraced Former Boston Archbishop Retires From Vatican*. Radio Boston http://radioboston. wbur.org/2011/11/21/former-boston-archbishop-retires Accessed 12 February 2012. Web.
20. Dr. Leonard Shlain. *The Alphabet versus the Goddess:The Conflict Between Word and Image*, Viking/Penguin, 1998.
21. According to SNAP (Survivors Network of those Abused by Priests) serious problems still exist regarding pedophile priests and attempts by the Catholic Church to hide those occurrences. http://www. snapnetwork.org. SNAP is the largest world-wide network supporting victims of religious abuse.

This organization also works to "change laws or legal practices that obstruct justice or protect predators" and provides support groups and prevention education through local chapters. Their national and international conferences feature top experts in this field.

22. Caroline Muir with permission. www.divine-feminine.com and www.carolinemuir.com
23. Joan Heartfield with permission. www.talkinghearts.com
24. Donna DeNomme "Listen to the Call" 6/17/2006 from Talking to Goddess, a women's anthology edited by D'vorah J. Grenn. CA: The Lilith Institute, 2009.
25. Rainer Marie Rilke, Letters to a Young Poet. The Modern Library, 1984, p.92 with permission.
26. Carl Jung. The Red Book, WW.Norton & Company, 2009, p. 314 with permission.

Chapter Three:
27. Helen Schuman "A Course in Miracles" T-19,I. P2;1 with permission from Foundation of Inner Peace.
28. Victor Frankl was a neurologist and psychiatrist as well as a Holocaust survivor. His most famous work is called, Man's Search for Meaning, Simon & Schuster, 1959.
29. I studied Lakota teaching through a group called Koda Maka led by a man of native descent under the tutelage of elders on the Pine Ridge Reservation. This was many years ago. An internet search for the name Koda Maka brought up a myriad of sites, none of which are related to the group I studied/practiced with. With great respect and sincere appreciation, I note what for me was a time of pivotal teaching with long-lasting results.
30. Sandra Ingerman. Soul Retrieval: Mending the Fragmented Self. Harper Collins, 2006, p.18 with permission.
31. Malidoma Somé. Ritual: Power, Healing, and Community. Penguin Compass, 1993, p.12, with permission.
32. Ibid, p. 22.
33. Mircea Eliade. Rites and Symbols of Initiations: The Mysteries of Birth and Rebirth. Spring Publications, 1005, p. xx. www.springjournalandbooks.com with permission.
34. Maureen Murdock. The Heroine's Journey: Woman's Quest for Wholeness. Shambhala, 1990, p.159.
35. Malidoma Somé. Ritual: Power, Healing, and Community, p.18 with permission.
36. Quoted with permission from Signposts to Elsewhere by Yahia Lababidi, p. 72. http://www.janestreet.org/press/signpostsfore.html
37. Carl Jung. Fundamental Questions of Psychotherapy, Princeton University Press, 1951.
38. Manly Palmer Hall. Healing: The Divine Art. Philosophical Research Society, 1943.
39. Quote by Louise Hay provided with permission.
40. Brief excerpt from p.79 from The Art of Living by Epictetus, A New Interpretation by Sharon Lebell. Copyright ©1995 by Sharon Lebell. Reprinted by permission of HarperCollins Publishers.

Chapter Four:
41. Depth Psychology is the study of the human psyche—conscious and unconscious.
42. MUSA: Museo Subacuatico de Arte. "El arte de la Conservacion" http://www.musacancun.com Accessed 20 January 2012. Web.
43. Note: the healing properties of blue glass have been referred to by many practitioners of various modalities including Dr. Ihaleakala Hew Len, the psychiatrist made famous for his use of the ancient Hawaiian Ho'oponopono method for healing.
44. Mirriam-Webster Online Dictionary http://www.mirriam-webster.com/dictionary/victim Accessed 1 November 2011. Web.
45. Matthew Fox. Original Blessing: A Primer in Creation Spirituality, Bear & Co, 1983, p.136.
46. Amy Berg. Deliver Us From Evil Directors Jacob Kusek and Jens Schlosser, Lionsgate, 2006. DVD.
47. Barbara Hand Clow. Chiron: Rainbow Bridge Between the Inner & Outer Planets. Llewellyn's Modern Astrology Library, 1994 with permission.
48. "Love after Love" from COLLECTED POEMS 1948-1984 by Derek Walcott. Copyright © 1986 by Derek Walcott. Reprinted by permission of Farrar, Straus and Giroux, LLC.

49. J.R. Haule. "The Naked Sword" *Divine Madness: Archetypes of Romantic Love*. Shambala, 1990. p.29. With permission from www.fisherkingpress.com.

50. Alexis DeTocquevell. *Democracy in America*. Translated Henry Reeve. Ed. Phillips Bradley. Alfred A. Knopf, 1954, Vol 2.

51. Donna DeNomme. *The Old Woman and the Basket* written to represent "personal peace." Peace Program 2010.

Chapter Five:

52. Louise Hay. *You Can Heal Your Life* Hay House, 1999. Page 198 reprinted with permission.

53. Frawley-O'Dea/Goldner. *Predatory Priests, Silenced Victims*. Page 103 – 109 with permission.

54. Mark D. Jordon. "The Confusion of Priestly Secrets" *Predatory Priests, Silenced Victims*. Frawley-O'Dea/Goldner, p.245 with permission.

55. Ibid, p.246.

56. Ibid, p.246-247.

57. Fr. Patrick Doyle, A.W.R. Sipe, and Patrick J. Wall. *Sex, Priests, and Secret Codes: The Catholic Church's 2,000 – Year Paper Trail of Sexual Abuse*. Los Angeles: Volt Press, 2006, p.230 with permission.

58. Ibid, p.237.

59. Edward F. Edinger *Ego and Archetype*, Shambhala Publications, 1992.

60. Leon Festinger. A *Theory of Cognitive Dissonance*. Stanford University Press, 1957.

61. John Grohol. *Cognitive Dissonance: Progress on a Pivotal Theory in Social Psychology* American Psychological Association blog: Washington, D.C. http://psychcentral.com/blog/archives/2008/10/19/fighting-cogntive-dissonance-the-lies-we-tell-ourselves. Accessed 13 January 2012. Web.

62. Jordon "Clericalism and Catholic Clergy Sexual Abuse," in *Predatory Priests, Silenced Victims*. Frawley-O'Dea/ Goldner, p.231 with permission.

63. Marion Woodman. "Beloved Enemy: A Modern Initiation" *The Pregnant Virgin: A process of psychological transformation*. Toronto, Canada. Inner City Books, 1985, p.188 with permission.

64. Laura Simms is an internationally-acclaimed storyteller and humanitarian, www.laurasimms.com.

65. Donna DeNomme. *Let Me Tell You A Story* 12/11/11. Written the morning after a lunar eclipse, during a week-end intensive, *The Alchemy that Opens the Heart of Mercy* facilitated by Laura Simms.

66. Edinger, *Ego and Archetype*, p.103.

67. Julia Cameron. *The Artist's Way: A Spiritual Path to Higher Creativity*. Jeremy P. Tarcher/Putnam, 1992.

Chapter Six:

68. Brief excerpt from p.290 from GODDESSES IN EVERYWOMAN by JEAN SHINODA BOLEN. Copyright ©1984 by Jean Shinoda Bolen, M.D. Reprinted by permission of HarperCollins Publisher.

69. Catherine T Keller. *God and Power: Counter-apocalyptic Journey*. Augsburg Books, 2005, p.135.

70. Carl Jung. *Memories, Dreams, Reflections*. Random House, 1961, p.184.

71. Leon J Podles. *Sacrilege, Sexual Abuse in the Catholic Church*. Baltimore, Maryland: Crossland Press, 2007 with permission http://crosslandfoundation.org, podles.org and bishopaccountability.org.

72. Doyle, Sipe, and Wall. *Sex, Priests, and Secret Codes* with permission from p.224.

73. For more information about Ernest Holmes, you can read The Science of Mind by Ernest Holmes, Dodd, Mead and Company, 1938, or visit www.milehichurch.org. Mile Hi Church also has a weekly on-line ministry. The Centers for Spiritual Living have international locations www.csl.org and a monthly magazine, published since 1927, www.scienceofmind.com.

74. Woodman. "Beloved Enemy: A Modern Initiation" *The Pregnant Virgin*. With permission from p.190.

75. Refer to http://www.scenicusa.net/090210.html or St. Malo Retreat Center: Chapel on the Rock (Facebook page) to determine the current status of this beautiful retreat center and chapel which has sustained a devastating fire (2011) and then Estes Park flood (2013).

76. You can see photos of El Sanctuario de Chimayo on their website www.elsanctuariodechimayo.us.

77. Material excerpted from the book, LIKE A TREE, ©2011 by Jean Shinoda Bolen with permission from Red Wheel/Weiser, LLC Newburyport, MA and San Francisco, CA www.redwheelweiser.com.

78. Bob Simon interviews Sister Pat Farrell: 60 Minutes broadcast Sunday, March 17, 2013.

79. "Sister Simone Campbell: Vatican Reprimand 'Like A Sock In The Stomach'" by Eyder Peralta in The Two-Way —NPR's News Blog Accessed 4/20/12.

80. Reprinted from *World as Lover, World as Self* (1991) by Joanna Macy with permission from Parallax Press, Berkeley, California, www.parallax.org.

81. Notes shared with permission from a radio broadcast, *Dreams, Visions, and Realities*, on Global Spirit January 22, 2012 with Dr. Stephen Aizenstat. http://www.lintv.org/globalspirit/dreams or www.dreamtending.com for general info on Dr. Aizenstat.

82. Deepak Chopra. *The Soul Hypothesis* (part 4), http://archive.chopra.com/wordsdeepakarchives?page=9, p.152. Accessed 12 October 2013. Web.

Chapter Seven:

83. Verse 36 {excerpt of 8 lines} from THE WAY OF LIFE ACCORDING TO LAO TZU EDITED by WITTER BYNNER. Copyright 1944 by Witter Bynner; renewed © 1972 by Dorothy Chauvenet and Paul Horgan. Reprinted by permission of HarperCollins Publishers.

84. Reprinted from *Call Me by My True Names* (1999) by Thich Nhat Hanh with permission from Parallax Press, Berkeley, California, www.parallax.org.

85. With permission from Coleman Barks. "Out Beyond" *A Year with Rumi: Daily Readings* and *The Essential Rumi*, HarperCollins, 2006.

86. With permission from Carl Studa. Public statement. Practitioner Huddle January 28, 2012.

87. With permission from Rev. Barry Ebert. "Stand in the Flame" original lyrics, iTunes.

88. With permission from Madisyn Taylor. Best-selling author, co-founder and editor-in-chief of the Daily Om, www.dailyom.com.

89. Melody Beattie has contributioned to the field of abuse and trauma with classic best-sellers *Codependent No More* (Hazledon Foundation, 1987) and *The Language of Letting Go* (1990) www.melodybeattie.com.

Chapter Eight

90. Ingerman. *Soul Retrieval.* With permission from HarperOne, p.18.

91. Woodman. *The Pregnant Virgin.* With permission p.182.

92. Donna DeNomme. *Hades Story,* August 2011.Written for Dr. Safron Rossi's Foundations of Myth course. Pacifica Graduate Institute: Fall 2011.

93. I want to be absolutely clear that I am in no way condoning abuse or saying that the perpetrator does the victim "a favor" by causing the abuse. Let's continue to loosen any stark black-and-white thinking about wrong and right or horrible and good, and accept that even in the worst of times, there is a most important treasure to be discovered. When you tap the inner resilience that comes from deep within you, you discover that you are strong beyond measure. After all, you already lived through the trauma.

94. Marion Woodman. *The Pregnant Virgin.* With permission from p.182.

95. The *Mundis Imaginalis* section is directly influenced by the writing of Henry Corbin and Tom Cheetham.

96. Tom Cheetham. *The World Turned Inside Out: Henry Corbin and Islamic Mysticism.* Spring Journal Books, 2003, p.57, www.springjournalandbooks.com with permission.

97. Excerpt from "Little Gidding" from FOUR QUARTETS by T.S. Eliot. Copyright 1940 by Houghton Mifflin Harcourt Publishing Company; Copyright © renewed 1968 by T.S. Eliot. Reprinted by permisssion of Houghton Mifflin Harcourt Publishing Company. All rights reserved.

The Path Leads Home

Something eternal, something with greater meaning,
begins to shine through the dark veil of earthly existence.

~ Marie-Louise von Franz

We can never really escape ourselves.

~ Donna DeNomme

I have been told that I needed to write about my past. There is no way, I thought . . . .

But some things in our lives go beyond our personal choice to a greater purpose. It was through a strange and synchronistic series of events, like with most of life's grand schemes, that I found myself writing with an abandon that navigated around all of my resistance, and the greater purpose made itself known.

The first opening peeked through a couple of years ago during a meditation welcoming in the new year, when I spontaneously, and distinctly, felt and "saw" two exquisite white birds rise from deep within my High Heart. They stretched and moved through my throat, pushing their way forcibly out through my mouth, flying freely airborne as I heard a voice of conviction say,

"Your wound has become your strength."